The MULTIPURPOSE COOKBOOK

Lucille Barber · Helen Dore
Catherine Redington · Jeni Wright

TREASURE PRESS

Above Pork paprikash with soured cream (page 30)

First published in Great Britain in 1985 by
Octopus Books Limited for the Electricity Council
under the title *The Electric Cookbook*

This edition published in 1989 by
Treasure Press
Michelin House
81 Fulham Road
London SW3 6RB

ISBN 1 85051 352 X

Produced by Mandarin Offset in Hong Kong

· CONTENTS ·

NOTES:

For all recipes, quantities are given in both metric and imperial measures. Follow either set but *not a mixture of both*, as they are not interchangeable.

All spoon measurements are level. 1 tablespoon = 15 ml. 1 teaspoon = 5 ml.
All eggs are sizes 3 or 4 (standard).

When using any electrical appliance always refer to the manufacturer's instructions. The recipes in this book have been tested on electric cookers with conventional ovens. When using a fan oven or non-British oven, timings may vary from those given in this book.

✳ denotes special freezing instructions

≋ denotes special microwave instructions

COOKING METHODS

Whether you use your cooker to create a
snack or a banquet, it can carry out
all the principal cooking techniques.

Roasting: Fast cooking in the oven; traditionally the best method for cooking large joints of meat. Roasting should produce particularly good crisp results, by browning and sealing in all the natural juices.

Grilling: Usually tender foods such as steaks and fish, cooked under direct heat. When grilling meat, the secret lies in quick sealing of the outside—so always preheat the grill before use.

Frying: Fast cooking by direct contact with heat. Particularly suitable for cooking tender foods that do not require long, slow cooking. Usually a little fat is used which prevents the food from sticking to the pan.

Deep-fat frying: Another fast process in which food is cooked by being immersed in hot fat. More delicate foods such as fish and poultry are often given a protective batter or egg-and-crumb coating to ensure that the outsides do not burn before the insides are cooked through.

Baking: Moderate cooking at lower temperatures in the oven—of anything from tougher cuts of meat, which require longer slower cooking, to delicate custards and, of course, cakes and pastries.

Braising and pot-roasting: The slow cooking of meat and/or vegetables in a covered pot in the oven or on the hob. Long steady cooking makes the most of tougher cuts of meat as well as bringing out full flavours of goods—particularly vegetables. The hob provides constant low temperatures, as does the invaluable purpose-built electric slow-cooker, which is also a remarkably economic means of cooking.

Boiling, poaching and steaming: Controllability is important for cooking foods at varying temperatures: be it a fast rolling boil for cooking vegetables and pasta; or a gentle simmer for the poaching of delicate foods; such as eggs and fish which require a steady temperature just below that of boiling. In steaming, the food is cooked above rapidly boiling water, thereby reducing loss of nutrients and retaining the shape and colour of foods.

Chilled Tomato and Mint Soup

SERVES 4

25 g (1 oz) butter

2 onions, chopped

2 sticks celery, chopped

2 rashers streaky bacon, rinded and chopped

2 × 397 g (14 oz) cans tomatoes, sieved

2 tablespoons tomato purée

300 ml (½ pint) chicken or
vegetable stock

few drops Worcestershire sauce

salt and black pepper

2 tablespoons chopped fresh mint

TO GARNISH:
4 teaspoons natural yogurt
fresh mint sprigs

Melt the butter in a large saucepan and fry the onions, celery and bacon for 5 minutes without browning. Add the tomatoes, tomato purée, stock, Worcestershire sauce and salt and pepper and bring to the boil. Lower the heat, cover the pan and simmer for 15 minutes. Sieve or place in a blender or food processor and blend until smooth. Leave to cool for 30 minutes to 1 hour.

Stir in the fresh mint and adjust the seasoning. Chill in the refrigerator.

Serve in chilled soup bowls, with a teaspoon of yogurt swirled into each and garnished with a sprig of fresh mint.

Note: Mint can be chopped quickly and easily in a food processor.

Serving suggestions: Serve with crispy fried, garlic-flavoured croûtons. For a light summer lunch, serve with French Country Pâté (page 11) and crusty wholemeal bread.

Variation: Use fresh basil to replace the mint. Single cream can be substituted for the natural yogurt for a richer flavour.

✴ Pack in a rigid container allowing a 1 cm (½ inch) headspace. Freeze for up to 3 months. Thaw overnight in the refrigerator.

≋ Microwave on DEFROST for 20–25 minutes breaking down the block as it thaws. Chill in the refrigerator before serving.

Left Chilled tomato and mint soup

5

Creamed Spinach and Nutmeg Soup

SERVES 4

25 g (1 oz) butter

1 bunch spring onions, finely chopped

450 g (1 lb) fresh spinach, chopped or
225 g (8 oz) frozen chopped spinach, thawed

300 ml (½ pint) milk

300 ml (½ pint) chicken stock

salt and black pepper

½ teaspoon ground nutmeg

4 sprigs fresh parsley

2 strips pared lemon rind

1 × 142 ml (5 fl oz) carton double or whipping cream

TO GARNISH:
2 tablespoons chopped fresh parsley
4 tablespoons grated Parmesan cheese

Melt the butter in a large saucepan over moderate heat. Add the spring onions and fry for 3 minutes. If using fresh, stir in the spinach and cook for 3 minutes until wilted. Stir in the thawed spinach, if using frozen, milk, stock, salt, pepper, nutmeg, parsley and lemon rind and bring to the boil. Lower the heat, cover the pan and simmer gently for 30 minutes.

Remove lemon rind and sieve the soup or place in a blender or food processor and blend until smooth.

Return to a clean pan. Stir in the cream and heat gently without boiling. Adjust the seasoning.

Just before serving, pour into individual warmed soup bowls and garnish each with chopped fresh parsley and a spoonful of Parmesan cheese.

✳ Pack in a rigid container allowing a 1 cm (½ inch) headspace. Freeze before adding the cream for up to 3 months. Thaw overnight in the refrigerator or for 4 hours at room temperature. To serve, reheat gently to boiling point. Stir in the cream and heat through without boiling.

≈ Microwave on HIGH for 8–10 minutes, breaking down the block as it thaws. Allow to stand for 5 minutes. Stir in the cream and reheat on HIGH for 4–6 minutes, stirring once.

Left Corn and crab chowder;
Right Beef and barley warmer

Corn and Crab Chowder

SERVES 6

450 g (1 lb) potatoes, peeled and diced
salt
50 g (2 oz) unsmoked streaky bacon rashers, rinded and diced
2 onions, finely chopped
1 heaped teaspoon paprika
450 ml (¾ pint) hot chicken stock
300 ml (½ pint) milk
1 × 170 g (6 oz) can crabmeat
1 × 298 g (10½ oz) can creamed sweetcorn
2 tablespoons lemon juice
1 × 142 ml (5 fl oz) carton whipping cream
black pepper
2 tablespoons snipped chives, to garnish

Boil potatoes in salted water for 5 minutes. Drain.

Fry the bacon in a large saucepan without added fat, until lightly browned, Add the onions and fry for 3–4 minutes or until the onions are soft and translucent. Sprinkle in the paprika and stir for 30 seconds. Stir in the stock, milk and any juices from the can of crabmeat. Bring to the boil, stirring. Add the potatoes, lower the heat and simmer for 7–10 minutes, or until the potatoes are tender. Stir in the creamed sweetcorn and the remaining ingredients, adding pepper to taste. Heat through thoroughly but do not boil. Serve in soup bowls and garnish with snipped chives.

✳ Pack in a rigid container allowing a 1 cm (½ inch) headspace. Freeze before adding the cream and chives, for up to 3 months. To serve, reheat gently from frozen. When thawed, bring to the boil. Lower the heat and simmer for 2 minutes. Stir in the cream and heat through without boiling.

≈ Microwave on HIGH for 8–10 minutes, breaking down the block as it thaws. Allow to stand for 5 minutes. reheat on HIGH for 10 minutes, stirring once. Stir in the cream and allow to stand for 3 minutes.

Beef and Barley Warmer

SERVES 4

25 g (1 oz) butter
450 g (1 lb) shin of beef, trimmed and cubed
1 onion, cut into eighths
1.2 litres (2 pints) beef stock
salt and black pepper
2 carrots, sliced
1 leek, sliced
175 g (6 oz) turnip, diced
3 tablespoons pearl barley
2 tablespoons chopped fresh parsley, to garnish

Melt the butter in a large saucepan over moderate heat. Add the meat and fry, stirring, to brown on all sides. Add the onion, stock, and salt and pepper. Cover and simmer gently for 1½ hours.

Add the vegetables and barley and simmer for a further 1 hour or until the barley is tender. Skim any fat from the surface of the soup. Garnish with parsley.

✳ Pack in a rigid container allowing a 1 cm (½ inch) headspace. Freeze for up to 3 months. Thaw overnight in the refrigerator. To serve, reheat gently to boiling point.

≈ Microwave on HIGH for 8–10 minutes, breaking down the block as it thaws. Allow to stand for 5 minutes. Reheat on HIGH for 8–10 minutes, stirring once.

MELBA TOAST
Lightly toast slices of white bread and remove the crusts. Split the toasts through the middle. Toast the uncooked surfaces under a preheated hot grill.

FANCY CROÛTONS
Toast white bread and cut out small fancy shapes using aspic cutters.

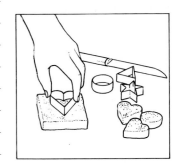

Alternatively, fry the bread on both sides in a little sunflower oil. Allow to cool slightly then cut out the fancy shapes.

CLEANING LEEKS

Leeks need to be cleaned thoroughly before use, as soil can sometimes remain lodged between the leaves.

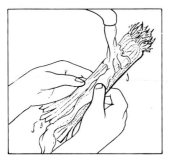

Split the leeks lengthways; hold under cold running water, gently separating the leaves to free any soil.

Below Four meats salad

Pipo Crème Leeks

SERVES 4

4 leeks, split lengthways, washed and cut in half
25 g (1 oz) butter
25 g (1 oz) flour
300 ml (½ pint) milk
black pepper
225 g (8 oz) Pipo Crème cheese, rinded and diced
3 tablespoons grated Parmesan cheese

Oven temperature: 180°C (350°F), Gas Mark 4

Put the leeks in a steamer and cook gently for 10 – 15 minutes or until they have softened.

Melt the butter in a saucepan. Add the flour and cook, stirring, for 2 minutes. Gradually stir in the milk and bring to the boil. When the sauce has thickened, remove from the heat, season with pepper and add the Pipo Crème cheese; stir until melted.

Arrange the leeks in a shallow ovenproof dish and cover with sauce. Sprinkle with Parmesan cheese; bake for 25 minutes or until bubbling and golden.

✳ Freeze cooked for up to 3 months. To serve, cover with foil and cook at 180°C (350°F) Gas Mark 4, for 30 minutes. Remove foil and cook for 15 minutes.

≈ Microwave on DEFROST for 8 minutes to thaw. Allow to stand for 5 minutes. Microwave on HIGH for 5–8 minutes to reheat.

Four Meats Salad

SERVES 4

75 g (3 oz) pasta noodles, such as tagliatelle
50 g (2 oz) sliced cooked ham
50 g (2 oz) sliced cooked silverside
50 g (2 oz) sliced cooked tongue
50 g (2 oz) sliced salami
1 carrot, peeled, cut into thin 5 cm (2 inch) strips
2 cocktail gherkins, cut into thin slices
black pepper
fresh coriander or parsley sprigs, to garnish

CROÛTONS:
50 g (2 oz) butter
½ clove garlic, crushed
2 × 1 cm (½ inch) thick slices white bread, cut into
1 cm (½ inch) cubes
pinch of salt
pinch of ground coriander

DRESSING:
4 tablespoons fresh orange juice
3 tablespoons olive oil
1 teaspoon whole grain mustard
½ teaspoon sugar
½ teaspoon dried mixed herbs
salt and black pepper

To make the croûtons, melt the butter in a frying pan. Add the garlic and then the bread and fry, turning frequently, until the croûtons are crisp and golden. Toss in the salt and coriander. Keep warm.

Bring a large saucepan of salted water to the boil and boil the pasta for 10–12 minutes until just tender but still firm to the bite. Drain and keep hot.

Slice the meats into thin 5 cm (2 inch) long strips and mix them together with the carrot and gherkins. Season with pepper. Mix into the hot pasta.

To make the dressing, place all the ingredients in a screw-top jar with salt and pepper to taste, and shake thoroughly. Pour the dressing over and toss well.

Serve the salad on individual plates garnished with croûtons and fresh coriander or parsley sprigs.

Note: The dressing can be prepared in advance and kept in the refrigerator for up to 1 day.

✳ Not suitable for freezing.

Deep-fried Broccoli

SERVES 4

25 g (1 oz) plain flour

pinch of salt

black pepper

pinch of cayenne

2 spears broccoli, cut into small florets

1 egg, beaten

100 g (4 oz) dry white breadcrumbs

oil, for deep-frying

DIP:
150 ml (¼ pint) mayonnaise
2 tablespoons tomato purée
dash Tabasco sauce
salt and black pepper

Mix the flour, salt, pepper and cayenne in a shallow dish. Dip the broccoli heads in the seasoned flour and shake off any excess. Then dip into the beaten egg and finally in the breadcrumbs to coat evenly.

Heat the oil in a deep-frying pan to 180°–190°C (350°–375°F) or a cube of stale bread dropped into the oil browns in 30 seconds. Drop the florets, a few at a time, into the oil and fry for 1–2 minutes or until crisp and golden. Remove with a slotted spoon and drain on kitchen paper. Keep warm until all the florets have been cooked.

Blend together the mayonnaise, tomato purée, Tabasco and seasoning. Serve with the broccoli.

✳ Not suitable for freezing.

Sautéed Scallops with Chives and Ginger

SERVES 4

2 teaspoons light soy sauce

1 tablespoon dry sherry

2.5 cm (1 inch) piece fresh root ginger, peeled and finely chopped

1 shallot, finely chopped

1 tablespoon fresh snipped chives

black pepper

1 tablespoon oil

12 large scallops, cleaned, or thawed if frozen

15 g (½ oz) butter

TO GARNISH:
lemon slices
fresh coriander leaves

Mix the soy sauce, sherry, ginger, shallot, chives, pepper and oil together. Put the scallops in a bowl, pour over the mixture and leave to stand, turning occasionally, for up to 1 hour.

Melt the butter in a large frying pan and add the scallops with the marinade. Fry, turning once, for 5 minutes or until just tender.

Serve hot, garnished with lemon wedges and coriander leaves.

Serving suggestion: Serve with plenty of hot whole-meal toast.

✳ Not suitable for freezing.

Top Deep-fried broccoli;
Bottom Sautéed scallops with chives and ginger

9

Shrimp-stuffed Mushrooms

SERVES 4–6

625 g (1¼ lb) large flat mushrooms

2 teaspoons lemon juice

100 g (4 oz) carrots, diced

120 ml (4 fl oz) chicken stock

15 g (½ oz) butter

1 tablespoon plain flour

salt and black pepper

pinch of grated nutmeg

pinch of curry powder

100 g (4 oz) peeled prawns, thawed if frozen

100 g (4 oz) ham, diced

100 g (4 oz) Edam cheese, diced

1 small red pepper, cored, seeded and diced

100 g (4 oz) Parmesan cheese, grated

Oven temperature: 220°C (425°F), Gas Mark 7

Trim the stalks from the mushrooms, chop and reserve. Sprinkle the caps with the lemon juice and place, gill sides up, in a greased baking dish.

Place the carrots in a saucepan with the stock and bring to the boil. Lower the heat, cover the pan and cook gently for 8–10 minutes. Drain and reserve the stock.

Melt the butter in a saucepan. Sprinkle in the flour and cook, stirring, for 1 minute. Stir in the reserved stock. Season to taste with salt and pepper, nutmeg and curry powder. Add the carrots, prawns, ham, Edam, red pepper and chopped mushroom stalks. Bring to the boil, stirring constantly, and remove from the heat.

Fill the mushroom caps with the mixture and spoon any remaining mixture between the mushrooms. Sprinkle with the Parmesan cheese and bake for about 12 minutes, until golden and bubbling. Serve immediately.

Serving suggestions: This dish makes a delicious *hors d'oeuvre* or, served with French bread and a salad, an appetizing main course.

✳ Not suitable for freezing.

Asparagus and Smoked Salmon Flan

SERVES 6

175 g (6 oz) plain flour

pinch of salt

100 g (4 oz) butter, chilled and diced

1 teaspoon dried dill

1 egg yolk

about 1 tablespoon iced water

FILLING:
175 g (6 oz) asparagus spears
100 g (4 oz) smoked salmon trimmings, chopped
3 eggs
200 ml (7 fl oz) double cream
1 teaspoon lemon juice
1 teaspoon dried dill
salt and black pepper

sprigs of fresh dill, to garnish

Oven temperature: 200°C (400°F); then: 180°C (350°F); Gas Mark 6; then: Gas Mark 4

Sift the flour with the salt into a mixing bowl. Add the butter and rub in with the fingertips until the mixture resembles fine breadcrumbs. Stir in the dill and the egg yolk, and enough iced water to mix to a fairly stiff dough. Turn on to a floured surface and knead lightly until smooth. Roll out the pastry and use to line a lightly oiled 23 cm (9 inch) flan tin. Chill well.

Prick the base and sides of the dough and line with greaseproof paper and baking beans. Bake 'blind' for 10 minutes, then remove the paper and beans and return to the oven for a further 5 minutes. Remove from the oven and set aside. Reduce the oven temperature to 180°C (350°F), Gas Mark 4.

To make the filling, steam the asparagus for 5 minutes and drain on kitchen paper. Scatter the smoked salmon trimmings in the pastry case, then arrange the asparagus on top in a pinwheel design.

Put the eggs in a bowl with the cream, lemon juice, dill, and salt and pepper to taste; beat well to mix. Pour into the flan, taking care not to disturb the asparagus.

Bake for 30–40 minutes or until the filling is golden brown and just set. Test with a skewer inserted at the centre; if it comes out clean, the flan is ready. Remove from the oven; garnish with a dill sprig.

Note: Frozen asparagus can be used instead of fresh. Thaw and drain, but do not steam, before using.

✳ Open freeze until firm then pack in a rigid container. Freeze for up to 4 months. Thaw at room temperature for 2–3 hours to serve cold. Reheat at 180°C(350°F), Gas Mark 4 for 15–20 minutes.

≋ Stand on kitchen paper. Microwave on HIGH for 5–6 minutes to thaw and reheat. Allow to stand for 3 minutes.

LINING A FLAN RING

Place the flan ring on a baking sheet.

Press the pastry into the ridges.

Roll off the surplus pastry.

French Country Pâté

SERVES 6–8

450 g (1 lb) chicken livers, roughly chopped

225 g (8 oz) pork belly, rinds and bones removed and roughly chopped

100 g (4 oz) sausagemeat

8–10 rashers streaky bacon, rinded

MARINADE:
6 tablespoons brandy
1 tablespoon port
2 tablespoons dry sherry
1 garlic clove, thinly sliced
1 tablespoon chopped fresh thyme or 1 teaspoon dried thyme
1 bouquet garni
pinch of grated nutmeg
salt and black pepper

TO GARNISH:
celery
radishes
lemon wedges

Oven temperature: 220°C (425°F), Gas Mark 7

Combine the marinade ingredients with salt and pepper to taste in a large bowl. Mix in the chicken livers, pork belly and sausagemeat. Cover and leave to marinate in the refrigerator for 24 hours, turning occasionally.

Stretch the bacon rashers with the back of a knife, then use to line the base and sides of a 450–750 g (1–1½ lb) terrine or loaf tin.

Discard the bouquet garni and spoon the marinated meat into the tin and smooth the surface. Cover with greaseproof paper and foil. Place the terrine in a roasting pan and pour in boiling water to come halfway up the sides. Bake for 1¾–2 hours until cooked through.

Remove the terrine from the roasting pan and leave until completely cold. Cover with fresh foil and put a weight on top. Chill in the refrigerator until firm.

Serving suggestion: Serve cut in slices garnished with celery, radishes and lemon wedges. Alternatively serve with toast or French bread.

✳ Freeze for up to 4 months. Thaw at room temperature for about 6 hours.

≈ Microwave on DEFROST for 12 minutes to thaw. Allow to stand for 15–20 minutes.

Left Asparagus and smoked salmon flan; **Right** French country pâté

French Bread Pizzas

SERVES 4–8

1 French stick

4 tablespoons tomato purée

1–2 teaspoons dried mixed herbs

1–2 cloves garlic, crushed (optional)

4 tomatoes, sliced

100 g (4 oz) salami, rinded and sliced

8 rashers streaky bacon, rinded and chopped

2 tablespoons capers

100 g (4 oz) Gruyère cheese, grated

Oven temperature: 200°C (400°F), Gas Mark 6
Cut the bread in half lengthways and cut each half into 4 equal pieces. Spread the tomato purée over the cut surfaces. Sprinkle with herbs and garlic, if using.

Arrange the sliced tomatoes and salami on the bread. Lay some bacon pieces on top of each piece, sprinkle with the capers and top with the cheese.

Place on lightly oiled baking sheets and bake for 15 minutes. Serve hot.

Variations: Use Mozzarella cheese instead of the Gruyère, ham instead of salami, anchovies instead of bacon, and olives instead of capers.

✳ Not suitable for freezing.

Tex-Mex Chicken Livers

SERVES 4–6

1 tablespoon oil

1 large onion, thinly sliced

2 cloves garlic, crushed

1 × 397 g (14 oz) can tomatoes

1 tablespoon tomato purée

1 teaspoon dried mixed herbs

½–1 teaspoon chilli powder

1 fresh chilli, seeded and sliced (optional)

salt and black pepper

450 g (1 lb) chicken livers, trimmed and roughly chopped

1 tablespoon plain flour

25 g (1 oz) butter

100 g (4 oz) button mushrooms, sliced

150 ml (¼ pint) dry white wine

Heat the oil in a pan, add the onion and garlic and cook for 5 minutes, until translucent but not browned. Stir in the tomatoes with their juice. Bring to the boil and cook rapidly for 5 minutes. Stir in the tomato purée, herbs, chilli powder, chopped chilli, if using, and salt and pepper to taste. Simmer, uncovered, for 20 minutes or until the sauce is thick.

Coat the chicken livers with the flour. Melt the butter in a saucepan, add the chicken livers and fry, stirring, for 5 minutes or until lightly browned. Drain on kitchen paper, then add to the tomato sauce with the mushrooms and wine. Bring to the boil, lower the heat and cook for 5–7 minutes, until the livers are cooked. Serve with tortilla chips.

✳ Freeze for up to 2 months. To serve, reheat gently to boiling point.

≈ Microwave on DEFROST for 5 minutes, breaking down the block as it thaws. Allow to stand for 5 minutes. Reheat on HIGH for 3–4 minutes, stirring once.

Spaghetti alla Carbonara

SERVES 4

350 g (12 oz) spaghetti

salt and black pepper

4 eggs

4 tablespoons freshly grated Parmesan cheese

4 tablespoons milk or cream

1 tablespoon oil

225 g (8 oz) smoked streaky bacon, rinded and cut into short strips

Cook the spaghetti in a large saucepan of boiling salted water for 12–15 minutes, or according to packet instructions.

Meanwhile, mix the eggs in a bowl with the Parmesan, milk or cream and salt and pepper to taste.

Drain the spaghetti thoroughly. Heat the oil in the pan in which the spaghetti was cooked. Add the bacon and fry gently until it changes colour. Return the spaghetti to the pan and toss quickly to heat through and combine with the bacon. Transfer to a heated serving bowl and add the egg mixture. Toss again to coat the spaghetti in the egg and serve immediately.

Note: The eggs cook lightly in the heat of the spaghetti when the two are tossed together. Do not mix them over heat or the eggs will scramble.

Serving suggestion: For those who like it, extra grated Parmesan cheese can be handed round separately.

✳ Not suitable for freezing.

Opposite: Top Tex-Mex chicken livers; **Bottom** Spaghetti alla carbonara

13

Ratatouille Tarts

MAKES 8

175 g (6 oz) plain flour

75 g (3 oz) butter, chilled and diced

2 tablespoons grated Parmesan cheese

½ teaspoon dried mixed herbs

1 egg yolk

a little iced water

FILLING:
1 tablespoon oil
1 onion, diced
2 garlic cloves, crushed
1 small aubergine, diced
1 small red pepper, cored, seeded and diced
1 small yellow pepper, cored, seeded and diced
2 small courgettes, thinly sliced
225 g (8 oz) tomatoes, chopped
1 tablespoon each chopped fresh thyme, basil and
oregano or
1 teaspoon each of the dried herbs
salt and black pepper
2 eggs
1 × 142 ml (5 fl oz) carton single cream

Oven temperature: 180°C (350°F), Gas Mark 4
Sift the flour into a bowl. Add the butter and rub in
with the fingertips until the mixture resembles fine
breadcrumbs. Mix in the cheese, herbs, egg yolk and
enough water to make a fairly stiff dough. Knead
lightly until smooth. Wrap in clingfilm and chill in the
refrigerator for 30 minutes.

Roll out the dough on a floured surface and use to
line eight 10 cm (4 inch) tartlet tins. Prick the base and
sides of the dough and chill for 20 minutes.

To make the filling, heat the oil in a saucepan, add
the onion and garlic and fry gently for 5 minutes
without browning. Add the vegetables, herbs and salt
and pepper to taste and fry, stirring, for 1–2 minutes.
Lower the heat, cover and cook gently for 20 minutes.
Remove from the heat and leave to cool.

Spoon the cooled filling into the pastry cases. Beat
the eggs and cream together, season with salt and
pepper, then spoon over the filling.

Bake for 20–25 minutes or until the pastry is cooked
and the filling set. Remove from the oven and leave to
cool in the tins for 10 minutes then transfer to a wire
rack to cool completely.

Serving suggestions: Serve with steamed summer
vegetables or a mixed green salad.

✳ Open freeze the tarts until firm then pack in a rigid
container. Freeze for up to 4 months. Reheat from
frozen at 180°C (350°F), Gas Mark 4 for 30 minutes.

≈ Stand the tarts on kitchen paper. Microwave on
HIGH for 6–8 minutes to thaw and reheat.

Prawn Luncheon Vol-au-vent

SERVES 4

375 g (13 oz) puff pastry, thawed if frozen

1 egg, beaten

FILLING:
40 g (1½ oz) butter
1 small red pepper, cored, seeded and diced
3 tablespoons plain flour
300 ml (½ pint) milk
1 tablespoon dry sherry
Tabasco sauce, to taste
pinch of cayenne pepper
salt
1 × 198 g (7 oz) can sweetcorn, drained
50 g (2 oz) frozen peas, thawed
100 g (4 oz) cooked chicken, cubed
350 g (12 oz) peeled cooked prawns, thawed if frozen

Oven temperature: 230°C (450°F), Gas Mark 8
Divide the pastry into two and roll each into a 23 cm
(9 inch) circle. Place 1 circle on a dampened baking
sheet. Using a very sharp knife, lightly mark a criss-
cross pattern over the other circle, then cut a 15 cm
(6 inch) circle (lid) from the centre of it.

Brush the first circle with beaten egg and fit the
pastry ring on top of it. Brush the ring with beaten
egg. Place the smaller circle on a separate dampened
baking sheet and brush with egg.

Bake the pastry case and lid for 15 minutes until

Left Prawn luncheon vol-au-vent; **Right** Ratatouille tarts

puffed and golden. Transfer to a wire rack to cool.

Meanwhile, melt the butter in a saucepan. Add the red pepper and fry gently for 2–3 minutes. Add the flour and cook, stirring constantly, for 2 minutes.

Add the milk gradually, stirring to prevent lumps forming. Bring to the boil, then lower the heat and simmer for 2 minutes. Add the sherry, Tabasco sauce, cayenne, and salt to taste. Stir in the sweetcorn, peas, chicken and prawns and simmer until heated.

Put the vol-au-vent case on a dampened baking sheet and return to the oven for about 5 minutes or until hot. Transfer to a heated serving dish, pile the filling into the case and put the lid on top. Serve.

✱ Open freeze the cooked vol-au-vent case and lid until firm then pack in a rigid container. Freeze the filling, without the prawns, separately. Freeze both for up to 1 month. To serve, thaw case and filling for 1 hour at room temperature. Warm the case and lid on a baking sheet at 220°C (425°F), Gas Mark 7 for 10 minutes. Place the filling in a saucepan and heat to boiling point. Add the prawns and simmer until heated through.

≈ Microwave the filling on HIGH for 5–6 minutes, stirring once, to thaw. Allow to stand for 3 minutes then stir in the prawns. Pile the filling into the pastry case and put the lid on top. Microwave on HIGH for a further 3–4 minutes.

Irish Pasties

MAKES 4
375 g (13 oz) puff pastry, thawed if frozen
350 g (12 oz) lean chuck or skirt steak, diced
225 g (8 oz) potatoes, diced
½ large Spanish onion, chopped
2 tablespoons Guinness
1–2 teaspoons dried mixed herbs
salt and black pepper
beaten egg, to glaze

Oven temperature: 220°C (425°F), Gas Mark 7
Divide the pastry into 4 equal pieces and roll out each piece to a 20 cm (8 inch) circle. Mix the meat, potatoes, onion, Guinness and herbs; season.

Divide the mixture into 4 equal portions and spoon a portion into the centre of each pastry round. Dampen the edges of the pastry and draw up, into the centre. Pinch and crimp the edges, sealing well. Place on a baking sheet; chill for 30 minutes. Brush with egg and bake for 30 minutes until golden.

✱ Open freeze until firm then pack in a rigid container. Freeze up to 1 month. Bake from frozen in foil at 180°C (350°F), Gas Mark 4 for 20 minutes. Unwrap and cook for a further 15 minutes.

≈ Stand on kitchen paper. Microwave on HIGH for 2–3 minutes, rearranging once, to thaw and reheat.

15

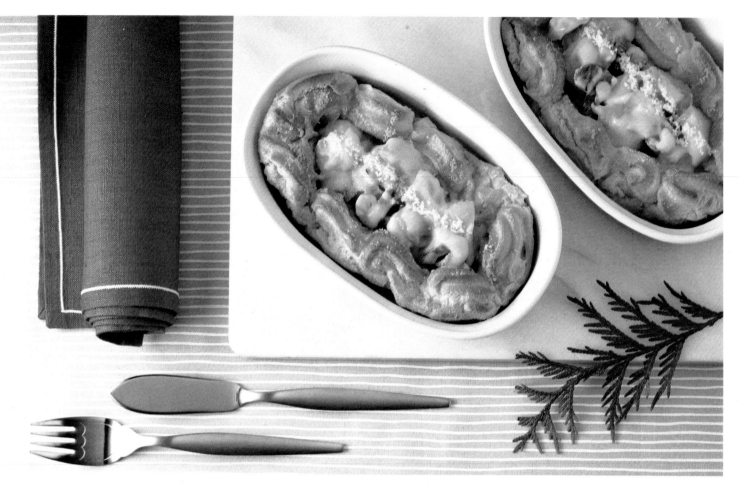

16

Above Smoked fish gougères

Minestrone

SERVES 4

3 tablespoons olive oil

25 g (1 oz) butter

2 small onions, finely chopped

1–2 garlic cloves, crushed

4 celery sticks, finely chopped

3 medium carrots, thinly sliced

1 × 397 g (14 oz) can chopped tomatoes

1.75 litres (3 pints) vegetable or chicken stock

½ teaspoon dried mixed herbs

½ teaspoon dried basil

salt and black pepper

1 × 283 g (10 oz) can red kidney beans, drained

75 g (3 oz) pastini (small soup pasta)

grated Parmesan cheese, to serve

Heat the oil and butter in a large saucepan. Add the onions, garlic and celery and fry gently for 10 minutes until soft and lightly coloured. Add the carrots and fry for a further 2–3 minutes. Add the tomatoes, stock, herbs, and salt and pepper to taste and bring to the boil. Cover and simmer for 25 minutes.

Add the beans and pasta and cook for a further 10 minutes or until the pasta is *al dente* (tender but firm to the bite). Taste and adjust seasoning before serving. Hand Parmesan cheese round separately.

Variations: No two Italian minestrones are alike – the Italian cook uses whatever is to hand in the kitchen, especially leftovers. This is a meatless version, but you can add diced bacon, ham or chicken if you like.

✳ Freeze before adding the beans and pasta for up to 3 months. Pack in a rigid container allowing a 1 cm (½ inch) headspace. To serve, reheat gently from frozen, adding a little stock or water to prevent sticking. When thawed, bring to the boil, add the beans and pasta and cook as in the recipe.

≈ Microwave on HIGH for 8–10 minutes, breaking down the block as it thaws. Reheat on HIGH for 4–5 minutes, stirring once. Add the beans and pasta, cover and cook for 10 minutes, stirring once. Allow to stand for 5 minutes before serving.

Smoked Fish Gougères

SERVES 4–6

130 g (5 oz) plain flour

salt

100 g (4 oz) butter

300 ml (½ pint) water

3–4 eggs

50 g (2 oz) mature or farmhouse Cheddar cheese, grated

2 tablespoons grated Parmesan cheese

FILLING:
450 g (1 lb) smoked haddock or cod fillets
600 ml (1 pint) milk
75 g (3 oz) butter
225 g (8 oz) button mushrooms, halved or sliced if large
50 g (2 oz) plain flour
100 g (4 oz) mature or farmhouse Cheddar cheese, grated
¼ teaspoon ground mace
black pepper

Oven temperature: 200°C (400°F), Gas Mark 6
First make the filling. Put the fish in a frying pan, pour in 150 ml (¼ pint) of the milk and enough water to just cover the fish. Bring slowly to boiling point, then cover and cook very gently for 15 minutes.

Meanwhile, melt 50 g (2 oz) of the butter in a saucepan, add the mushrooms and fry over moderate heat for 5 minutes. Remove with a slotted spoon and set aside.

Melt the remaining butter in the pan, sprinkle in the flour and cook, stirring, for 1–2 minutes.

Remove from the heat and gradually blend in the remaining milk. Bring to the boil, stirring, then lower the heat and simmer until thick. Add the cheese, mace, and pepper to taste, and stir until the cheese melts. Remove from the heat.

Drain the fish. Flake the flesh, discarding the skin and any bones. Fold the fish and mushrooms gently into the sauce. Set aside while making the choux pastry.

Sift the flour and a pinch of salt on to kitchen paper. Put the butter in a large saucepan with the water. Heat gently until the butter has melted, then bring to boiling point. Remove from the heat and immediately pour in the flour all at once. Beat vigorously until a smooth ball of dough is formed in the centre of the pan, then beat in the eggs a little at a time until the dough is firm, smooth and shiny (you may not need all 4 eggs). Beat in the Cheddar cheese.

Spoon the dough into a piping bag fitted with a large star nozzle. Pipe a deep border around the edges of 4–6 greased individual ovenproof serving dishes. Spoon the filling in the centre.

Sprinkle half the Parmesan cheese over the choux dough and bake for 20–25 minutes until the pastry is risen and golden brown. Serve hot with the remaining Parmesan cheese sprinkled over the filling.

Serving suggestion: Gougères make a very substantial lunch or supper dish for those with good appetites. Serve with a mixed salad or a tomato and fennel salad and dry French cider or white wine.

Variation: Use a mixture of prawns and white fish fillets instead of the smoked haddock. Diced cooked chicken also goes well with the mushrooms and cheese.

✱ Not suitable for freezing.

Cheese Soufflé

SERVES 4

40 g (1½ oz) butter

3 tablespoons plain flour

250 ml (8 fl oz) warm milk

75g (3 oz) mature Cheddar cheese, grated

salt and black pepper

pinch of cayenne pepper

pinch of grated nutmeg

4 egg yolks

5 egg whites

½ teaspoon cream of tartar

Oven temperature: 190°C (375°F), Gas Mark 5
Butter an 18 cm (7 inch) soufflé dish. Place the dish on a baking sheet.

Melt the butter in a saucepan, sprinkle in the flour and cook, stirring, over low heat for 1 minute. Gradually stir in the milk and cook for 2–3 minutes. Bring to the boil then remove from the heat and stir in the cheese and seasonings.

Beat in the egg yolks, one at a time. Whisk the egg whites with the cream of tartar until they form stiff peaks and fold into the cheese mixture. Pour the mixture into the prepared soufflé dish, knock the bottom of the dish lightly on the work surface to expel any large air pockets, and smooth the top of the soufflé. Quickly run a knife around the top of the mixture about 2.5 cm (1 inch) from the edge to make the soufflé rise evenly in a crown. Bake for about 25 minutes, until puffed up, golden brown on top and just firm. Serve at once.

Variations: Make a blue cheese soufflé using crumbled Stilton or Danish blue cheese instead of Cheddar. For a herb and cheese soufflé add 2 tablespoons chopped fresh herbs, such as parsley or basil, to the cheese sauce mixture.

✱ Not suitable for freezing.

17

Above Tarragon chicken crêpes

18

Opposite: Top Curried seafood scramble; **Bottom** Gorgonzola soufflé toasts

Gorgonzola Soufflé Toasts

SERVES 3–4

225 g (8 oz) Gorgonzola cheese

2 eggs, separated

black pepper

6 slices white bread, crusts removed

butter, for spreading

snipped chives, to garnish

Put the Gorgonzola cheese in a bowl with the egg yolks and pepper to taste. Mash until soft and mixed.

In a separate bowl, whisk the egg whites until stiff. Fold into the Gorgonzola mixture until well mixed.

Toast the bread lightly on one side only. Spread the untoasted side with butter, then top with the Gorgonzola mixture, leaving a narrow margin around the edges.

Put the toasts under a preheated hot grill for 1–2 minutes until puffed up and golden. Serve immediately, garnished with snipped chives.

Note: For speed, use an electric toaster to toast the bread; but be sure to toast on the lowest or lightest setting to avoid burning the edges or crusts.

Serving suggestion: Serve for a quick, impromptu evening snack or supper, with halved tomatoes dotted with butter, sprinkled with chopped basil and plenty of black pepper, and grilled.

Variation: If you find Gorgonzola cheese too sharp, use the sweeter, milder Dolcelatte instead.

✳ Not suitable for freezing.

Tarragon Chicken Crêpes

MAKES 8

100 g (4 oz) plain flour

pinch of salt

1 egg

300 ml (½ pint) milk

oil, for frying

FILLING:
25 g (1 oz) butter
25 g (1 oz) flour
300 ml (½ pint) milk
salt and black pepper
1 large avocado pear, cubed
juice of half a lemon
225 g (8 oz) cooked chicken, chopped
3 spring onions, sliced
1 teaspoon chopped fresh tarragon or
½ teaspoon dried tarragon

1 spring onion, to garnish

Oven temperature: 180°C (350°F), Gas Mark 4

Sift the flour with the salt into a bowl. Make a well in the centre and drop in the egg. Using a whisk, start beating the egg, gradually drawing in the flour and adding the milk a little at a time. Beat until smooth.

Heat an 18 cm (7 inch) frying pan over moderate heat, then brush very lightly with oil. Pour in sufficient batter just to cover the base, tilting the pan to spread evenly. Cook gently until the underside of the crêpe is golden. Toss or turn, using a spatula or palette knife, and cook on the other side. Slide on to a heated plate and keep hot. Cook the remaining crêpes in the same way, interleaving them with greaseproof paper, and keeping them warm in a low oven.

To make the filling, melt the butter in a saucepan and stir in the flour. Cook gently for 1 minute then gradually add the milk. Bring to the boil, stirring continuously, until the sauce has thickened. Season with salt and pepper. Combine the avocado with the lemon juice, stir in the chicken, onion and tarragon and season to taste. Stir gently into the sauce. Spread on each crêpe; roll up and arrange in an ovenproof dish. Cover with aluminium foil and heat in the oven for 15–20 minutes before serving. Garnish.

✳ Freeze the pancakes, before filling, interleaved with greaseproof paper, for up to 4 months. Do not freeze the filling. To serve, separate the pancakes and thaw at room temperature for 30 minutes. Then use as fresh pancakes.

≈ Do not separate pancakes. Microwave on DE-FROST for 6 minutes, turning twice. Allow to stand for 5 minutes, separate and use as fresh pancakes.

Curried Seafood Scramble

SERVES 4

65 g (2½ oz) butter or margarine

1 small onion, finely chopped

2 teaspoons garam masala

1 teaspoon ground turmeric

225 g (8oz) frozen peeled prawns

2 tomatoes, skinned and finely chopped

salt and black pepper

4 eggs

2 tablespoons cream or top of the milk

4 wholemeal or granary baps

TO GARNISH:
lime wedges
coriander leaves

Melt 25 g (1 oz) of the butter in a saucepan. Add the onion, garam masala and turmeric and fry gently, stirring frequently, for 5 minutes until the onion is soft.

Add the prawns and tomatoes with salt and pepper to taste. Increase the heat and stir-fry until the prawns have thawed. Continue stir-frying until all the liquid has evaporated.

Beat the eggs with the cream or milk and salt and pepper to taste. Melt a little of the remaining butter in a clean pan, pour in the egg mixture and cook gently, stirring, until the eggs are soft, creamy and scrambled.

Meanwhile, toast the baps until crisp. Spread with the remaining butter.

Fold the prawn mixture gently into the scrambled eggs off the heat. Pile on to the toasted baps, grind black pepper on top and garnish with lime wedges and coriander leaves. Serve immediately.

Notes: Be careful when scrambling eggs. Keep the heat low and remove from the hob *immediately* the eggs start to thicken – they will continue cooking off the heat with the heat from the pan. If you leave the pan on the hob too long, the eggs will go rubbery.

Garam masala is a blend of Indian spices, which usually combines cardamom seeds, coriander seeds, cumin seeds, cloves and peppercorns. It forms the base for many Indian dishes and is available from most supermarkets or good delicatessens.

Serving suggestion: Serve for a nutritious evening snack, or a weekend brunch dish.

Variations: Use drained bottled mussels or clams instead of the prawns, or drained canned crab or shrimps.

✱ Not suitable for freezing.

19

Pot Roast Pizzaiola

SERVES 4

2 tablespoons beef dripping or oil

1.5 kg (3 lb) boned, rolled and tied brisket of beef

2 small onions, thinly sliced

1–2 cloves garlic, roughly chopped (optional)

1 × 397 g (14 oz) can tomatoes

1 × 198 g (7 oz) can sweet red peppers (pimentos) in water, drained

300 ml (½ pint) beef stock

150 ml (¼ pint) full-bodied red wine (e.g. Côtes du Rhône)

1 teaspoon dried oregano

1 teaspoon dried basil

salt and black pepper

12–16 black olives, stoned

1–2 tablespoons capers, to taste

chopped fresh parsley, to garnish

Oven temperature: 170°C (325°F), Gas Mark 3

Heat the dripping or oil in a large flameproof casserole, add the beef and fry until browned on all sides. Remove and drain on kitchen paper.

Add the onions to the pan with the garlic, if using. Fry gently, stirring constantly, until soft. Add the tomatoes, peppers, stock, wine, herbs, and salt and pepper to taste. Bring to the boil, stirring, then return the beef to the pan.

Cover and cook in the oven for 2½–3 hours or until the meat is really tender. Stir in the olives and capers, taste and adjust the seasoning.

To serve, slice the meat into neat rounds and arrange overlapping on a warmed meat dish. Spoon some of the sauce over the meat; sprinkle with parsley. Serve the rest of the sauce separately in a warmed sauceboat.

Note: Brisket has an excellent flavour and succulent texture when cooked slowly with wine and strong flavourings as here, but it can be a fatty joint of meat. For best results, cook the day before required and leave in a cool place or the refrigerator overnight. The next day, simply skim or lift off any fat that has risen to the surface before reheating for serving.

✳ Freeze, covered with the sauce made without the olives and capers, for up to 3 months. Thaw overnight in the refrigerator. Add the olives and capers. Reheat gently on the hob until the rolled beef is heated through, about 15–20 minutes.

≈ Microwave on DEFROST for 10 minutes to thaw. Allow to stand for 10 minutes. Add the olives and capers. Microwave on HIGH for 10–12 minutes to reheat.

MAKING THE STILTON ROLL

Form the Stilton mixture into a cylinder, 2.5 cm (1 inch) in diameter; wrap in greaseproof paper and chill until hard.

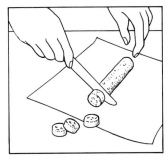

Just before cooking the steaks, cut the chilled roll into 1 cm (½ inch) slices.

20

Steak with Stilton and Walnuts

SERVES 4

6 tablespoons olive oil

2 tablespoons red wine or red wine vinegar

2 cloves garlic, crushed

4 rump or sirloin (porterhouse) steaks, trimmed of fat

175 g (6 oz) blue Stilton cheese

75 g (3 oz) shelled walnuts, finely chopped

1 teaspoon chopped fresh or ½ teaspoon dried sage

2 tablespoons red wine or port

salt and black pepper

sprigs of fresh sage, to garnish

Put the oil, wine or wine vinegar and garlic in a shallow dish, which is large enough to hold the steaks in a single layer. Mix with a fork until well combined. Add pepper to taste.

Place the steaks in the dish and brush with the marinade. Cover the dish and leave to marinate for at least 4 hours, preferably overnight. Turn the steaks in the marinade from time to time.

Crumble the cheese into a bowl. Add the walnuts, sage, wine or port, a little salt and plenty of pepper. Mash with a fork until well combined. Roll into a cylinder shape; wrap in greaseproof paper and chill in the freezer.

Cook the steaks under a preheated very hot grill for 2 minutes on each side for rare meat, 3 minutes for medium, 4 minutes for well-done. Brush with the marinade during grilling to ensure the steaks are juicy.

Remove the steaks from the grill and top with a slice of the chilled Stilton roll. Return to the grill for a further minute until melted and browned. Serve immediately, garnished with sage.

Note: The steaks can be left in the marinade in the refrigerator for up to 3 days—the longer they are left, the more tender they will be.

Serving suggestion: Serve with grilled halved tomatoes and a green salad or a fresh seasonal vegetable such as French beans or mange-tout peas.

✳ The steaks may be frozen in their marinade for up to 1 month. Thaw at room temperature for 3–4 hours. The Stilton roll may be frozen for 1 month; thaw for 1 hour in the refrigerator before use.

Beef Olives

SERVES 4

4 × 75 g (3 oz) thin slices of silverside or 'leg of mutton' of beef

2 tablespoons oil

150 ml (¼ pint) full-bodied red wine

300 ml (½ pint) beef stock

salt and black pepper

TO GARNISH:
chopped walnuts
chopped fresh parsley

STUFFING:
2 tablespoons oil
1 small onion, finely chopped
2 celery sticks, finely chopped
1 clove garlic, crushed (optional)
75 g (3 oz) fresh white breadcrumbs
50 g (2 oz) shelled walnuts, very finely chopped
50 g (2 oz) Parmesan cheese, grated
1 × 50 g (2 oz) can anchovy fillets in oil, drained and chopped
finely grated rind and juice of 1 lemon
2 tablespoons chopped fresh parsley
1 egg, beaten

Oven temperature: 170°C (325°F), Gas Mark 3
Put the slices of beef between 2 sheets of greaseproof paper. Beat with a meat mallet or rolling pin to flatten. Cut each slice in half. Set aside while making the stuffing.

Heat the oil in a small frying pan, add the onion, celery and garlic, if using, and fry gently, stirring, until softened. Transfer to a bowl, add the remaining stuffing ingredients with salt and pepper to taste and mix well.

Divide the stuffing equally between the slices of beef, placing it at one end of each slice. Roll the beef up around the stuffing, then tie with string or secure with wooden cocktail sticks.

Heat the oil in a large flameproof casserole, add the beef olives and fry over moderate heat until browned. Pour in the wine and stock, add salt and pepper to taste and bring to the boil.

Cover the casserole and bake for 2 hours or until the beef feels tender when pierced with a skewer. Sprinkle with walnuts and parsley before serving.

Note: The beef cut called 'leg of mutton' is boneless, from the thick rib of the animal. It is an inexpensive braising or slow roasting cut, with little fat.

Variation: Use all beef stock instead of the combination of red wine and stock, if the dish is not for a special occasion. Veal escalopes can be used instead of the beef, in which case it would be better to use white wine and chicken stock. For a special occasion, stir some cream into the sauce just before serving.

✳ Freeze for up to 3 months. Thaw overnight in the refrigerator. Reheat gently on the hob for about 20 minutes.

≋ Microwave on DEFROST for 20 minutes to thaw. Microwave on HIGH for 8–10 minutes to reheat, stirring once.

Above Steak with Stilton and walnuts

Suetcrust Steak and Stout Pies

MAKES 4

1 kg (2 lb) chuck steak, trimmed of fat and cut into small cubes

2 tablespoons plain flour

2 teaspoons dried mixed herbs

1 teaspoon English mustard powder

salt and black pepper

4 tablespoons oil

1–2 tablespoons Worcestershire sauce, to taste

1 × 275 ml (9 fl oz) can sweet stout

300 ml (½ pint) beef stock or water

16–20 button (pickling) onions, peeled and blanched in boiling water for 5 minutes

225 g (8 oz) button mushrooms, halved if large

SUETCRUST PASTRY:
225 g (8 oz) self-raising flour
1 teaspoon English mustard powder
1 teaspoon dried mixed herbs
1 teaspoon salt
100 g (4 oz) shredded suet
about 150 ml (¼ pint) water
beaten egg, to glaze

22

Below A Suetcrust steak and stout pie

Oven temperature: 170°C (325°F); then: 200°C (400°F); Gas Mark 3; then: Gas Mark 6

Put the beef in a polythene bag with the flour, herbs, mustard powder, and salt and pepper to taste. Close the bag and shake vigorously until the meat is thoroughly coated.

Heat half of the oil in a large flameproof casserole, add the beef and fry until browned on all sides. Add the Worcestershire sauce, stout and stock or water and bring slowly to the boil, stirring all the time. Cover and cook gently on the hob or in the oven for about 2 hours or until the beef is tender. Remove from the oven and leave until cold, preferably overnight.

About 1½ hours before you are ready to serve, make the suetcrust pastry. Sift the flour into a bowl with the mustard powder, herbs and salt. Stir in the shredded suet, then mix in enough water to make a smooth elastic dough. Knead on a floured surface.

Heat the remaining oil in a frying pan, add the onions and mushrooms and toss over moderate heat until lightly coloured on all sides. Remove with a slotted spoon and drain on kitchen paper.

Remove any fat from the surface of the beef mixture, then stir in the onions and mushrooms. Divide equally between 4 individual pie dishes, piling the mixture slightly higher than the rim of the dishes so that the pastry does not sink during baking.

Roll out the pastry on the floured surface and cut out 4 lids to fit the pie dishes. Place on top of the filling, moistening the rims of the dishes with water so that the pastry sticks. Brush with beaten egg to glaze, then make a small slit in the centre of each pie to allow the steam to escape.

Bake in a preheated 200°C (400°F), Gas Mark 6 oven for 45 minutes to 1 hour until the pastry is crisp and golden brown. Serve hot.

Note: The filling must be cold before the pastry is placed on top or the finished suetcrust will be soggy. It is much better to leave the filling overnight as this both improves the flavour and enables you to remove any traces of fat.

Serving suggestion: These traditional pies make a filling meal. Serve with side plates of carrots and broccoli, and creamed potatoes for those who are really hungry.

Variations: Instead of mushrooms, use a drained 105 g (3.66 oz) can of smoked oysters (but do not fry them with the onions). Steak and oyster pie was traditional in Victorian times, when fresh oysters were as cheap and plentiful as mushrooms are today, but today smoked oysters offer an inexpensive alternative. As an alternative to beef suet, use 'Suenut', a pure vegetable fat available from health food shops. It can be used in exactly the same way as beef suet, and gives light results.

✱ The cooked meat mixture can be frozen for up to 3 months. Thaw for about 6 hours at room temperature then make the pastry and continue with the recipe as above.

Somerset Beef and Chestnut Casserole

SERVES 4

2 tablespoons beef dripping or oil

1 medium onion, finely chopped

1 kg (2 lb) chuck steak, trimmed of fat and cut into large cubes

3 tablespoons plain flour

450 ml (¾ pint) beef stock

300 ml (½ pint) dry cider

2 tablespoons soft dark brown sugar

2 teaspoons dried mixed herbs

¼ teaspoon English mustard

salt and black pepper

4 medium carrots, thinly sliced

439 g (15½ oz) can whole chestnuts in water, drained

chopped fresh parsley, to garnish

Oven temperature: 170°C (325°F), Gas Mark 3
Heat the dripping or oil in a heavy flameproof casserole, add the onion and beef and fry, stirring constantly, over moderate heat until lightly browned.

Sprinkle in the flour and stir for 1–2 minutes until browned, then pour in the stock and cider. Bring slowly to the boil, stirring, then stir in the sugar, herbs, mustard and salt and pepper to taste.

Cover and cook in the oven for 2–2½ hours or until the beef is really tender.

About 1 hour before the cooking time is up, cook the sliced carrots in boiling salted water for 10 minutes. Drain and add to the casserole with the chestnuts for the remainder of the cooking time.

To serve, taste and adjust seasoning and transfer to a warmed serving dish or clean casserole. Sprinkle liberally with parsley and serve hot.

Serving suggestion: This hearty warming casserole makes a filling and nutritious meal in the winter served with jacket-baked potatoes or Braised red cabbage (page 49).

Variation: Brown ale or sweet stout can be used instead of cider, but the flavour of the finished dish will be stronger. Chuck steak is the best quality stewing cut of beef, but shin or leg of beef, which has more flavour than chuck, is also suitable for this dish – and less expensive. Shin tends to have more fat and sinews, so it is best to cook it the day before and remove the fat before reheating – this will produce a beautifully rich gravy.

✳ Freeze, without the chestnuts, for up to 3 months. Cook from frozen in a covered casserole in a 200°C (400°F), Gas Mark 6 oven for 1¼ hours until bubbling. Add the chestnuts for the last 15 minutes cooking time.

≋ Microwave on DEFROST for 20 minutes to thaw. Allow to stand for 5 minutes. Microwave on HIGH for 10–12 minutes to reheat, stirring once. Add the chestnuts for the last 5 minutes cooking time.

23

Below Somerset beef and chestnut casserole

Above Steak teriyaki, garnished with celery sticks

Spiced Scandinavian Meatballs

SERVES 4–6

350 g (12 oz) minced beef

350 g (12 oz) minced pork

100 g (4 oz) smoked streaky bacon, rinded and very finely chopped

75 g (3 oz) fresh breadcrumbs

1 small onion, grated

½–1 teaspoon ground allspice, to taste

2 eggs, beaten

salt and black pepper

2 tablespoons plain flour, for coating

50 g (2 oz) butter

1 tablespoon oil

150 ml (¼ pint) dry white wine

300 ml (½ pint) chicken stock

1 teaspoon fresh or ½ teaspoon dried dill

1 × 142 ml (5 fl oz) carton soured cream

chopped fresh dill or parsley, to garnish

Put the beef, pork and bacon in a large bowl with the breadcrumbs, onion and allspice. Mix with your hands until the ingredients are well combined. Bind the mixture with the beaten eggs, adding salt and pepper to taste.

With your hands, form the mixture into 20–24 meatballs. Coat in the flour seasoned with salt and pepper.

Melt the butter with the oil in a large flameproof casserole. Add the meatballs in batches and fry over high heat for about 7 minutes until browned on all sides. Remove with a slotted spoon and drain on kitchen paper.

Pour the wine and stock into the casserole and bring slowly to the boil, stirring to scrape up any sediment from the base of the pan. Add the dill, and salt and pepper to taste, then return the meatballs to the pan. Cover and simmer very gently for 30 minutes.

Remove from the heat and allow the sauce to settle for 5 minutes, then stir in about half of the soured cream. Drizzle the remaining cream over the top and sprinkle with dill or parsley. Serve hot.

Note: The mixture of minced beef and pork gives these meatballs a moist texture and good flavour. You can use all minced beef, but the end result will not be quite so successful. Minced veal or minced lamb would make a better alternative than using all beef.

Variation: For an everyday family meal, omit the wine and use all stock. Natural yogurt can be used instead of soured cream.

✳ Freeze, without the soured cream, for up to 3 months. Thaw at room temperature for about 4 hours. Reheat on the hob for about 20 minutes. Stir in the soured cream to serve as above.

≈ Microwave on DEFROST for 10 minutes to thaw. Allow to stand for 15 minutes. Microwave on HIGH for 10 minutes to reheat, stirring once. Stir in the soured cream to serve as above.

Mexican Chilli Cabbage Pie

SERVES 4–6

40 g (1½ oz) butter

1 tablespoon oil

1 medium onion, chopped

1 clove garlic, crushed (optional)

450 g (1 lb) minced beef

175 g (6 oz) long grain rice

2 tablespoons tomato purée

½ teaspoon chilli powder, to taste

¼ teaspoon sugar

salt and black pepper

450 ml (¾ pint) beef stock

14 light-coloured large cabbage leaves (from a Savoy or Celtic cabbage)

2 eggs, beaten

1 × 283 g (10 oz) can red kidney beans, drained

Oven temperature: 190°C (375°F), Gas Mark 5

Melt two-thirds of the butter with the oil in a heavy-based saucepan or flameproof casserole. Add the onion with the garlic, if using, and fry gently until soft but not coloured.

Add the minced beef and fry until it has changed colour, breaking up any lumps with a wooden spoon. Add the rice, tomato purée, chilli powder, sugar, salt and pepper to taste, then the stock. Bring to the boil, stirring, then lower the heat. Cover and simmer for about 20 minutes, stirring frequently, until the rice is tender and has absorbed the liquid.

Meanwhile, blanch the cabbage leaves in batches for 3 minutes in boiling salted water. Drain and pat dry with kitchen paper.

Remove the beef and rice mixture from the heat and set aside to cool slightly. Meanwhile, brush the inside of a 1.5–1.75 litre (2½–3 pint) round flame-proof dish with the remaining butter. Line the dish with cabbage leaves, overlapping them so that there are no spaces between and letting the cabbage overhang the edges.

Beat the eggs into the beef and rice mixture, then stir in the beans. Adjust seasoning. Spoon into the dish and level the surface. Cover with the remaining cabbage leaves, tucking in the edges, then bringing the overhanging leaves over the top to seal the filling like a pie. Brush with more butter.

Bake uncovered for 35–40 minutes until firm. Leave to stand at room temperature for 10 minutes, then turn out on to a warmed serving plate and cut into wedges like a cake. Serve hot.

Note: When selecting the cabbage leaves for this dish, remove the coarse outer leaves from a Savoy or Celtic cabbage and use the large, paler-coloured ones underneath. Brown long grain rice gives the pie a nutty texture, but will take 30–40 minutes to cook according to the variety.

Serving suggestions: With meat, rice and vegetables cooked together, there is no need to serve an accompaniment with this filling family supper dish. Hand round a bowl of soured cream for those who like it, or serve with a home-made tomato or cheese sauce.

Variation: For an interesting, golden-brown topping, turn the stuffed cabbage out on to a baking sheet and sprinkle with grated cheese. Place under a hot grill to brown.

✱ Not suitable for freezing.

Steak Teriyaki

SERVES 4

4 thick fillet steaks

4 cloves garlic

2.5 cm (1 inch) piece fresh root ginger, peeled

6 tablespoons soy sauce

4 tablespoons sake (Japanese rice wine) or dry sherry

a little oil, for brushing

sliced celery sticks, to garnish

Trim any fat off the fillet steaks, then cut the meat into thin slices, slicing across the grain. Place in a shallow dish, keeping the slices in the shape of the steak as much as possible.

Pound the garlic and ginger together in a mortar with a pestle, then mix with the soy sauce and saké or sherry. Pour over the steak, then cover the dish with clingfilm and leave to marinate in the refrigerator for 1–4 days. Turn the meat in the marinade occasionally during this time.

When ready to cook, let the steak come to room temperature for 1–2 hours. Thread the slices of steak on to bamboo skewers which have been soaked in cold water.

Brush the steaks lightly with oil and any marinade that has not been absorbed into the meat. Cook under a preheated very hot grill for about 2 minutes on each side, turning once. Serve immediately, garnished with sliced celery sticks.

Note: The longer the steak is left in the marinade the more tender it will be.

Variation: Rump steak can be used instead of fillet, but the cooking time will be longer. Cut the steak as thinly as possible.

✱ Freeze the steak in the marinade for up to 1 month. Thaw in the refrigerator for 1–2 days, then bring to room temperature and cook as above.

MAKING CHILLI CABBAGE PIE

Line the inside of the buttered dish with the blanched cabbage leaves, overlapping them so that there are no spaces between; allow the leaves to overhang the dish.

Pour the filling into the lined dish and cover with the remaining cabbage leaves, tucking in the edges and folding over the leaves around the edges. Brush with more butter before baking.

25

Lamb Pasanda

SERVES 4

6 cardamom pods

4 whole cloves

2 teaspoons coriander seeds

6 black peppercorns

50 g (2 oz) butter

1 large onion, thinly sliced

2.5 cm (1 inch) piece root ginger, peeled and crushed

2 cloves garlic, crushed

2 teaspoons ground turmeric

1 teaspoon salt

1.25 kg (2½ lb) lamb fillet, trimmed of fat and cut into cubes

2 × 150 g (5.29 oz) cartons natural yogurt

TO GARNISH:
25 g (1 oz) flaked almonds
25 g (1 oz) seedless raisins
sprig of fresh coriander

Crush the cardamom pods, cloves, coriander and peppercorns in a mortar with a pestle. Melt the butter in a flameproof casserole, add the onion and ginger and fry gently until soft.

Add the garlic, the crushed spices, turmeric and salt. Continue frying gently, stirring constantly, for a further 5 minutes.

Add the meat, increase the heat and stir to coat in the spice mixture. Fry until browned on all sides. Add three-quarters of the yogurt, 1 tablespoon at a time, stir-frying after each addition.

Lower the heat, cover and simmer, stirring occasionally, for about 1 hour or until the lamb is tender.

Transfer to a serving dish, drizzle the remaining yogurt over the top and garnish with the nuts, raisins and coriander. Serve immediately.

Note: Lamb fillet comes from the middle neck and is boned, ready for casseroling or braising, by the butcher. It is the perfect lamb for curries, casseroles and kebab dishes because it is leaner than shoulder but more moist than leg. Ask your butcher for it a few days in advance because there is only a small amount of fillet from each animal and he may not always have sufficient in stock.

If possible, make this dish a day ahead of serving as the flavour improves on reheating and the oil separates out from the sauce in true Indian style.

Serving suggestion: This mild, Indian-style dish is deceptively rich. Serve with a dish of natural yogurt, Naan bread and spinach cooked with onions, butter, paprika and coriander. Plain boiled rice, or potatoes added to the spinach dish, will help offset the richness of the meat.

✳ Freeze, without the garnish, for up to 1 month. Thaw overnight in the refrigerator before reheating in a 180°C (350°F), Gas Mark 4 oven for 40 minutes or until bubbling.

≈ Microwave on DEFROST for 20 minutes to thaw. Allow to stand for 5 minutes. Microwave on HIGH for 10–12 minutes to reheat, stirring once.

26

Below Lamb pasanda, served with yogurt and Naan bread

Lamb and Spinach Gratin

SERVES 4–6

2 tablespoons oil

1 large onion, finely chopped

2 cloves garlic, crushed

450 g (1 lb) minced lamb

2 tablespoons tomato purée

1 teaspoon ground allspice

salt and black pepper

450 g (1 lb) frozen leaf spinach

1 × 150 g (5.29 oz) carton natural yogurt

2–3 tablespoons grated Parmesan cheese, for sprinkling

CHEESE SAUCE:
50 g (2 oz) butter or margarine
65 g (2½ oz) plain flour
600 ml (1 pint) milk
100 g (4 oz) Feta cheese, crumbled
1 egg, beaten

Oven temperature: 190°C (375°F), Gas Mark 5
Heat the oil in a flameproof casserole, add the onion and garlic and fry gently for 5 minutes until soft but not coloured. Add the lamb and continue frying until browned, breaking up any lumps.

Stir in the tomato purée, allspice, and salt and pepper to taste and then cook very gently for 15 minutes, stirring frequently.

Meanwhile, make the cheese sauce. Melt the butter or margarine in a saucepan, add the flour and cook, stirring, for 1–2 minutes. Remove from the heat and blend in the milk a little at a time. Bring to the boil, stirring, then simmer for 3 minutes until thick and smooth. Add the Feta cheese, a little salt and plenty of pepper and continue simmering and stirring until the cheese has melted. Remove from the heat.

Remove the lamb mixture from the heat and skim or blot the surface with kitchen paper to remove excess fat. Thaw the spinach in a pan over low heat, stirring frequently, until dry.

Stir the yogurt into the lamb, then remove half of the mixture from the casserole. Add a little salt and plenty of pepper to the spinach, then spread half over the lamb in the casserole. Repeat these 2 layers.

Stir the egg into the cheese sauce, then pour over the spinach and sprinkle with the Parmesan cheese. Bake for 25–30 minutes or until golden and bubbling. Leave to settle for 5–10 minutes, then sprinkle extra cheese on top before serving.

Note: Add salt sparingly, because Feta is a salty cheese. Before using Feta, taste a little and check the saltiness. If you think it is very salty, soak it in cold water for about 1 hour, then drain.

Serving suggestion: This dish makes a very substantial family supper dish. Serve with Greek retsina wine and a tomato, onion and black olive salad.

Variation: You can, of course, use minced beef instead of lamb, but lamb gives a more authentic Middle Eastern flavour.

✳ Freeze, unbaked, in the casserole for up to 2 months. Cover with foil and bake from frozen at 190°C (375°F), Gas Mark 5 for 30 minutes. Uncover and cook for a further 30 minutes.

≋ Microwave on DEFROST for 25 minutes. Allow to stand for 10 minutes. Microwave on HIGH for 5–7 minutes to reheat.

Marinated Lamb Kebabs

SERVES 4

1 kg (2 lb) lean boneless lamb (fillet, leg or shoulder), cut into cubes

1 large onion, quartered, separated and cut in pieces

1 large green or red pepper, cored, seeded and cut into pieces

12 bay leaves

MARINADE:
6 tablespoons natural yogurt
4 tablespoons olive oil
2 tablespoons lemon juice
1 small onion, grated
2 cloves garlic, crushed with 1 teaspoon salt
3 tablespoons chopped fresh coriander
black pepper

TO SERVE:
chopped fresh coriander
lemon wedges

First make the marinade. Put all the ingredients into a large bowl, with plenty of pepper. Stir briskly to mix. Add the cubes of lamb and mix well to coat in the marinade. Cover the bowl and leave to marinate for at least 4 hours, preferably overnight.

When ready to cook, thread the cubes of lamb on to oiled kebab skewers, alternating with the onion and pepper pieces and the bay leaves. Cook under a preheated moderate grill for about 20 minutes until tender, turning the skewers frequently to ensure even cooking. Sprinkle with fresh coriander before serving and accompany with lemon wedges.

✳ Freeze the lamb in the marinade for up to 1 month. Thaw in the refrigerator for 24 hours before threading on to skewers to grill.

≋ Microwave on DEFROST for 8–10 minutes to thaw. Allow to stand for 10–15 minutes before threading on to skewers to grill.

27

Right French-style roast lamb, served with a selection of seasonal vegetables

MAKING FRENCH-STYLE ROAST LAMB

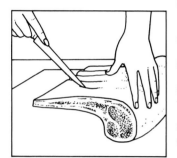

Trim about 6 cm (2½ inches) of meat from the end of each bone.

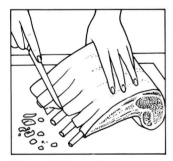

Scrape the bones clean.

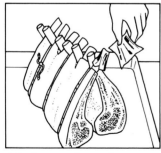

Join the two pieces of meat, skin-side out, so that the bones criss-cross along the top. Tie the joint securely with string. Wrap the tip of each bone with aluminium foil to prevent it from burning during roasting.

French-style Roast Lamb

SERVES 4

2 racks of lamb, each with 6 cutlets, chined
3 tablespoons olive oil
salt and black pepper
4 tablespoons Dijon mustard
4 cloves garlic, crushed
2 tablespoons chopped fresh rosemary
sprigs of fresh rosemary, to garnish

Oven temperature: 200°C (400°F); then: 180°C (350°F); Gas Mark 6; then: Gas Mark 4

Trim the fat off the ends of the lamb bones with a sharp knife, then scrape the bones clean. There should be about 5 cm (2 inches) of bone exposed.

Stand the racks fat-side uppermost in a lightly oiled roasting tin. Interlock the bones if you wish, to make one joint (a 'Guard of Honour'). Rub the olive oil into the fat, along with plenty of salt and pepper.

Mix together the mustard, garlic and rosemary and brush or spread all over the oiled lamb. Leave to stand at room temperature for 1–4 hours before cooking.

Sprinkle the joint with more salt and pepper, then roast for 15 minutes. Lower the oven temperature to 180°C (350°F), Gas Mark 4 and roast for a further 1–1¼ hours. Serve hot, garnished with sprigs of fresh rosemary.

Note: A rack of lamb is the best end of neck of lamb; it is important to ask your butcher to chine, or remove the backbone from, the rack, otherwise you will find it difficult to cut into chops for serving.

Serving suggestion: The ends of the bones of lamb can be garnished with cutlet frills or tiny cherry tomatoes for a special occasion. Make a gravy from the meat juices, adding a splash of white wine or Pernod if you have a bottle open, and serve in the French style with simple vegetable dishes – new potatoes tossed in butter and herbs, French beans, matchstick carrots, courgettes or mange-tout peas.

Variation: For a crunchy coating, press about 8 tablespoons fresh breadcrumbs into the mustard mixture just before roasting.

✳ Not suitable for freezing.

Seville Pork Chops

SERVES 4

15 g (½ oz) butter
1 tablespoon vegetable oil
4 pork chops (loin or fillet end of leg)
1 small onion, finely chopped
finely grated rind of 1 orange
150 ml (¼ pint) freshly squeezed orange juice
2 tablespoons lemon juice
4 tablespoons ginger marmalade
1 cinnamon stick
2 dessert apples, peeled, cored and sliced
100 ml (3½ fl oz) chicken stock or dry white wine

TO GARNISH:
1 orange, sliced
1 dessert apple, cored and sliced
pared rind of 1 orange

Melt the butter with the oil in a large heavy-based saucepan. Add the chops and fry over moderate heat until lightly coloured on all sides. Remove with a slotted spoon and drain on kitchen paper.

Add the onion to the pan and fry gently until soft but not coloured. Add the orange rind, orange and lemon juices, half of the marmalade, the cinnamon stick, apples and stock or wine.

Bring to the boil, stirring, then lower the heat and return the chops to the pan. Cover and simmer gently for 45–60 minutes or until the chops are tender.

Remove the chops from the pan with a slotted spoon and keep hot. Discard the cinnamon stick. Sieve the cooking liquid or place in a blender or food processor and blend until smooth. Return to the rinsed-out pan, taste and adjust seasoning and keep over low heat while preparing the garnish.

Melt the remaining marmalade in a small pan, then add the orange and apple slices. Turn the fruit to coat in the marmalade.

Cover the bases of 4 warmed dinner plates with pools of the smooth sauce, then place the chops in the centre. Arrange the orange and apple slices and the pared orange rind beside each chop and serve immediately.

Note: For this *nouvelle-cuisine*-style dish, try to choose lean chops if possible. Loin chops should have the rind and fat trimmed off. Fillet end of leg looks best if it is trimmed of fat then formed into a neat shape with wooden cocktail sticks (which can be quickly removed before serving). Some supermarkets which have a 'continental' butchery section, sell *médaillons* or pork escalopes, which are excellent for this dish; allow a shorter cooking time.

Serving suggestion: In *nouvelle-cuisine* style, serve crisply cooked vegetables on separate side plates.

Choose from tiny new potatoes tossed in chopped fresh herbs, small broccoli spears, carrot matchsticks, French beans, mange-tout peas and creamed spinach with nutmeg.

Variation: Use different kinds of marmalade in the sauce for a change – lime marmalade would go very well.

✳ Freeze the chops in the unsieved cooking liquid for up to 3 months. Thaw overnight in the refrigerator, then continue with the recipe.

≋ Microwave on DEFROST for 20 minutes to thaw. Allow to stand for 5 minutes. Continue with the recipe.

Below Seville pork chops, garnished with orange and apple slices

Loin of Pork with Dried Fruits

SERVES 4–6

2 kg (4½ lb) loin of pork, boned, with rind scored

450 g (1 lb) mixed dried fruit (e.g. pitted prunes, apricots, apple rings, pineapple, mango)

100 g (4 oz) dried whole figs

1 teaspoon ground cinnamon

salt and black pepper

150 ml (¼ pint) dry white wine

2 tablespoons redcurrant jelly

Oven temperature: 220°C (425°F); then: 180°C (350°F), Gas Mark 7; then: Gas Mark 4

Put the loin of pork, rind side down, on a board or work surface. With a sharp knife, make a slit underneath the 'eye' of the loin for the stuffing.

With kitchen scissors, cut three-quarters of the dried fruit and figs into small pieces. Mix with the cinnamon and salt and pepper. Fill the slit in the pork with the dried fruit and figs, pressing it together with your fingers. Roll up the meat around the stuffing and then tie with string at regular intervals.

Put the joint, rind side down, in a roasting pan into which it just fits. Add the wine and enough water to cover the rind and fat of the pork.

Roast for 20 minutes, then turn the joint over and sprinkle 2 teaspoons salt over the rind. Roast for a further 40 minutes to 1 hour, or until the crackling is crisp. Lower the heat to 180°C (350°F), Gas Mark 4 and roast for a further 2 hours 20 minutes, adding the remaining dried fruit and figs for the last 30 minutes. Do not baste the joint at all during roasting or the crackling will not crisp.

Transfer the joint to a carving board and leave to stand in a warm place for about 15 minutes (this makes the meat easier to carve). Remove the fruit from the cooking liquid with a slotted spoon and set aside.

Carefully transfer the roasting pan to the hob and boil rapidly until the cooking liquid reduces slightly. Stir in the redcurrant jelly, with salt and pepper to taste. Heat gently, stirring until the jelly has melted, then return the fruit to the pan and heat through. Pour into a warmed sauceboat and serve with the pork.

Note: Exotic whole and halved dried fruits are available from health food shops, and most of them do not have added sugar. Choose fruits with contrasting colours such as apricots and prunes, as these give the stuffing an attractive appearance.

Serving suggestion: Serve for a special Sunday lunch, with Middle Eastern-style saffron rice and courgettes.

✱ Not suitable for freezing.

Pork Paprikash with Soured Cream

SERVES 4

3 tablespoons oil

2 large onions, thinly sliced

1 kg (2 lb) pork stewing meat (e.g. hand, shoulder, sparerib, leg), trimmed of excess fat and cubed

1 tablespoon paprika

¼ teaspoon sugar

1 × 397 g (14 oz) can Passata (sieved Italian tomatoes)

450 ml (¾ pint) chicken stock or 300 ml (½ pint) stock and 150 ml (¼ pint) dry white wine

2 bay leaves

salt and black pepper

1 × 142 ml (5 fl oz) carton soured cream, at room temperature, to serve

Heat 2 tablespoons of the oil in a heavy flameproof casserole. Add the onions, cover the pan and fry very gently, stirring frequently, for 20 minutes or until soft.

Remove the onions with a slotted spoon and set aside. Heat the remaining oil in the pan, add the pork and increase the heat. Fry briskly until the meat is lightly browned on all sides.

Lower the heat and sprinkle in the paprika. Fry, stirring, for 1–2 minutes. Return the onions to the pan, add the sugar and meat and stir to mix, then pour in the tomatoes and stock (or stock and wine). Bring slowly to boiling point, then add the bay leaves and salt and pepper to taste.

Cover and simmer gently, stirring occasionally, for about 1½ hours until the pork is tender. Add more stock or water if the sauce becomes too thick.

Before serving, remove the bay leaves, taste and adjust the seasoning of the sauce. Serve hot, with the soured cream handed separately.

Note: Canned *Passata* is available at some large supermarkets. It is a very thick purée of tomatoes, excellent for making sauces and casseroles, and well worth buying to save you time and trouble. If you are unable to find it, use ordinary canned whole or chopped tomatoes and press through a sieve, then thicken with tomato purée according to taste.

Serving suggestions: With its thick, pungent sauce, this casserole makes a hearty main course. Serve with jacket baked potatoes or boiled brown rice. Choose a seasonal green vegetable such as purple sprouting broccoli or runner beans to go with this dish. Alternatively serve with a tossed green salad mixed with black olives.

Variations: Use chicken stock for an everyday meal, wine for a special occasion. To make the meat go further, add 225 g (8 oz) button mushrooms. Fry them

STUFFING A BONED LOIN OF PORK

Using a sharp knife, make a deep slit underneath the 'eye' of the loin.

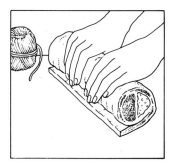

Fill the slit with the stuffing, pressing it well in. Roll up the meat and tie with string at regular intervals to secure.

in butter just before serving, then add to the casserole at the last minute.

✳ Freeze without the soured cream for up to 3 months. Thaw at room temperature for about 4 hours before gently reheating on the hob for about 20 minutes. Serve hot, with the soured cream handed separately.

≈ Microwave on DEFROST for 20 minutes to thaw. Microwave on HIGH for 8–10 minutes to reheat, stirring once. Serve hot, with the soured cream handed separately.

Oven-baked Honey Spareribs

SERVES 4

about 1.5 kg (3 lb) Chinese-style pork spareribs

2 teaspoons demerara sugar

1 teaspoon salt

SAUCE:
6 tablespoons clear honey
4 tablespoons demerara sugar
3 tablespoons frozen concentrated orange juice
2 tablespoons red wine vinegar
2 tablespoons soy or Worcestershire sauce
1 tablespoon tomato purée or ketchup
2 teaspoons Dijon mustard

Oven temperature: 200°C (400°F); then: 180°C (350°F), Gas Mark 6; then: Gas Mark 4
Cut the sheets of spareribs into single ribs, using kitchen scissors or a very sharp knife. Put them in a large roasting pan and sprinkle with the sugar and salt. Roast for 30 minutes. Meanwhile, put all the sauce ingredients in a saucepan and heat gently, until melted and bubbling.

Remove the pan of ribs from the oven, pour in the sauce and shake the pan to mix the sauce and meat cooking juices together. Return to the oven and roast for a further 30 minutes.

Remove the pan from the oven and turn the ribs over in the sauce. Reduce the oven temperature to 180°C (350°F), Gas Mark 4 and roast for a further 30 minutes or until the sauce has reduced to a thick glaze over the ribs. Serve hot.

Note: Chinese-style spareribs are cut from inside the thick end of the belly of pork, not to be confused with the thicker sparerib chops, which come from the neck end of the animal. Most butchers sell Chinese spareribs, although you may have to ask in advance, and some large supermarkets also sell them, both fresh and frozen.

Serving suggestions: To be enjoyed to the full, spareribs must be eaten with the fingers, so they're a good choice for family meals, and for informal entertaining. Provide plenty of paper napkins and finger bowls, and serve the ribs on their own with the sauce as it is difficult to eat vegetables at the same time. Follow with a Chinese stir-fried dish of noodles, beansprouts and other crisp vegetables.

✳ Not suitable for freezing.

Above Oven-baked honey spareribs, served with Chinese-style stir-fried vegetables.

Puff-top Veal and Ham in Cream Sauce

SERVES 4

4 veal escalopes, each weighing about 100 g (4 oz)

2 tablespoons plain flour

salt and black pepper

25 g (1 oz) butter

1 tablespoon vegetable oil

100 g (4 oz) button mushrooms, wiped and finely sliced

300 ml (½ pint) dry white wine

2 teaspoons tarragon mustard

½ teaspoon turmeric

1 × 368 g (13 oz) packet frozen puff pastry, thawed

beaten egg, to glaze

225 g (8 oz) thick slice of honey roast ham, cut into 2.5 cm (1 inch) cubes

1 × 142 ml (5 fl oz) carton double cream

sprigs of fresh tarragon, to garnish (optional)

Oven temperature: 220°C (425°F), Gas Mark 7

Put the escalopes between 2 sheets of clingfilm or greaseproof paper and beat out thinly with a meat mallet or rolling pin. Remove the film or paper and cut the veal into 2.5 cm (1 inch) squares.

Put the pieces of veal in a polythene bag with the flour, seasoned with salt and pepper. Shake the bag so that the veal is well coated in the flour.

Melt the butter with the oil in a flameproof casserole, add the mushrooms and fry, stirring constantly, over moderate heat for 5 minutes. Remove with a slotted spoon and set aside.

Add the veal to the pan (reserving the excess flour in the bag) and fry over moderate heat until lightly coloured on all sides. Remove with a slotted spoon and set aside on a plate.

Sprinkle the reserved flour into the pan and cook, stirring, for 1–2 minutes, then pour in the wine and bring to the boil.

Lower the heat, return the veal to the pan and stir in the tarragon mustard and turmeric. Cover and simmer gently, stirring occasionally, for 10–15 minutes until the veal is tender. Remove the veal from the cooking liquid with a slotted spoon and set aside on a plate.

Roll out the pastry on a floured surface and cut out four 11.5 cm (4½ inch) circles. Crimp the edges and make a small hole in the centre of each one with a skewer. Decorate with the pastry trimmings, sticking them on with water.

Place the circles on a dampened baking sheet and brush lightly with beaten egg to glaze. Bake for 15 minutes or until golden.

Meanwhile, return the casserole to the heat and boil the cooking liquid rapidly to reduce slightly. Lower the heat, return the veal and mushrooms to the pan, then add the ham and cream and heat through gently. Taste and adjust seasoning. Divide the veal and ham mixture equally between 4 individual plates and top with the pastry circles at an angle. Garnish with sprigs of fresh tarragon, if available, and serve immediately.

Serving suggestion: Easier to serve and eat than a large pie or individual pies, this veal dish makes an excellent dinner-party main course. Serve with crisply cooked green vegetables such as French beans, mange-tout peas and broccoli. A chilled, dry white Bordeaux wine would go well with the veal, both in the sauce and as a drink to serve with the meal.

✳ Not suitable for freezing.

Veal Goulash with Caraway Dumplings

SERVES 4–6

2 tablespoons oil

2 medium onions, thinly sliced

1–1.25 kg (2–2½ lb) pie veal, trimmed of fat and cut into cubes

1 tablespoon paprika

1 teaspoon caraway seeds

1 green pepper, cored, seeded and sliced

1 red pepper, cored, seeded and sliced

1 × 397 g (14 oz) can tomatoes

300 ml (½ pint) chicken stock

salt and black pepper

225 g (8 oz) button mushrooms, halved or sliced if large

soured cream, to serve

DUMPLINGS:
450 g (1 lb) potatoes
2 teaspoons caraway seeds
about 100 g (4 oz) plain flour
1 egg, beaten

Heat the oil in a large flameproof casserole. Add the onions and fry gently, stirring occasionally, for about 10 minutes, until soft and lightly coloured.

Add the veal and fry until lightly coloured on all sides, then add the paprika and caraway seeds. Fry, stirring, for a few minutes more.

Add the peppers, tomatoes, stock and salt and pepper to taste. Bring slowly to the boil, then lower the heat. Cover the casserole and simmer very gently for 1½ hours.

MAKING CARAWAY DUMPLINGS

Roll each piece of dough into a ball between floured palms. Leave to rest for 30 minutes.

Gently drop the dumplings into boiling, salted water and stir slowly, until they rise to the surface. Simmer for 1–2 minutes. Lift the dumplings out of the water using a slotted draining spoon.

33

Left Veal goulash with
caraway dumplings

Meanwhile, make the dumplings. Cook the potatoes in their skins in boiling salted water for 20–25 minutes until tender. Drain and leave until cool enough to handle, then peel off the skins. Mash the potatoes in a bowl with the caraway seeds, then turn on to a well-floured work surface. Work in half of the flour and the egg with the fingers until a soft, smooth dough is formed.

Divide the dough in half and roll each half into a long sausage shape, using more flour if the dough is sticky. Cut each roll into about 12 pieces and then roll into balls. Sprinkle the work surface with more flour and leave the dumplings to rest for about 30 minutes.

Meanwhile, add the mushrooms to the veal and cook for a further 30 minutes until the veal is tender.

When ready to serve, bring a very large pan of salted water to the boil and drop in the dumplings. Stir very gently, bring the water back to the boil and continue stirring until the dumplings rise to the surface. Leave to simmer for 1–2 minutes.

Transfer the goulash to a warmed serving dish and spoon a few of the dumplings on top. Serve the rest in a separate warmed dish and hand a bowl of soured cream separately.

Serving suggestion: Potato dumplings are traditionally served with goulash in Austria, but you can serve plain boiled or creamed potatoes instead.

✳ Freeze the goulash only (without the dumplings and soured cream) for up to 3 months. Thaw at room temperature for 4–6 hours, then reheat on the hob until bubbling. Proceed as above.

≋ Microwave on DEFROST for 20 minutes to thaw and reheat. Allow to stand for 5 minutes. Microwave on HIGH for 8–10 minutes to reheat, stirring once.

Sweetbreads with Spinach and Gruyère

SERVES 4

750 g (1½ lb) frozen lambs' sweetbreads, thawed

salt and black pepper

1 onion, chopped

1 carrot, chopped

1 celery stick, chopped

1 bouquet garni

300 ml (½ pint) dry cider, white wine or chicken stock

32 young fresh spinach leaves

about 150 ml (¼ pint) milk or cream

40 g (1½ oz) butter or margarine

40 g (1½ oz) plain flour

100 g (4 oz) Gruyère cheese, grated

1 teaspoon mustard powder

¼ teaspoon grated nutmeg

about 8 tablespoons dried breadcrumbs

Oven temperature: 200°C (400°F), Gas Mark 6

Put the sweetbreads in a bowl of salted water and leave to soak for 3–4 hours, changing the water several times during soaking, until they are white.

Drain the sweetbreads and rinse under cold running water. Blanch in boiling salted water for 2–3 minutes, then drain and leave until cool enough to handle. Peel off the skin, and cut away all gristle and stringy tissue.

Slice the sweetbreads thinly. Place in a saucepan with the onion, carrot, celery and bouquet garni. Pour in the cider, wine or stock, add salt and pepper to taste and bring to the boil. Lower the heat, cover and simmer for 10–15 minutes until tender.

Meanwhile, remove the large stalks from the spinach leaves. Blanch the leaves in boiling water for 10 seconds. Drain and dry on kitchen paper.

Remove the sweetbreads from the cooking liquid with a slotted spoon. Strain the cooking liquid into a measuring jug and make up to 450 ml (¾ pint) with milk or cream.

Melt the butter or margarine in a clean saucepan, add the flour and cook, stirring, for 1–2 minutes. Blend in the measured liquid a little at a time, then bring to the boil, stirring constantly. Lower the heat and simmer for 3–4 minutes. Stir in two-thirds of the cheese, the mustard powder, nutmeg and salt and pepper to taste. Simmer until the cheese has melted. Remove from the heat.

Put 2 spinach leaves, one on top of the other, on a board and place a few sweetbread slices at 1 end. Sprinkle with salt and pepper. Roll up the leaves around the sweetbreads, then place, join side down, in a buttered ovenproof dish. Repeat with the remaining spinach and sweetbreads to make 16 rolls.

Pour over the cheese sauce. Mix the remaining cheese with the breadcrumbs and sprinkle over the top. Bake for 15 minutes until golden. Serve hot.

Note: Lambs' sweetbreads are available from most large supermarkets; some butchers also stock them, or you may order them in advance. Calves' sweetbreads are also sold, but they take longer to prepare because they must be pressed after blanching.

✻ Freeze in the dish, before baking, for up to 3 months. Bake from frozen, allowing double the cooking time.

≈ Microwave on DEFROST for 20 minutes to thaw. Microwave on HIGH for 6–8 minutes to reheat.

Calves' Liver with Sage and Marsala

SERVES 4

4 thin slices calves' liver, total weight about 450 g (1 lb)

2 tablespoons plain flour

4 teaspoons rubbed fresh sage or 2 teaspoons dried sage

salt and black pepper

50 g (2 oz) butter

1 tablespoon olive oil

4 tablespoons Marsala wine

Spread the flour out on a plate and mix in the sage with salt and pepper to taste. Dip and coat the liver pieces in the flour mixture.

Melt the butter with the oil in a large, heavy-based frying pan until foaming. Add the liver and fry over moderate heat for 2–3 minutes on each side, turning once. Remove with a fish slice or spatula and arrange on a warmed serving platter.

Pour the Marsala into the pan and increase the heat. Let bubble for 1–2 minutes, stirring and scraping up the sediment from the base of the pan. Pour over the liver and serve immediately.

Note: Calves' liver, although expensive compared with lambs' and pigs' liver, is so tender that it quite literally melts in the mouth, and is therefore well worth the extra expense. Take great care not to overcook it, or you will ruin its delicate texture. To be enjoyed at its best, it should be served rare like steak. Marsala is a fortified Italian wine, which the Italians use frequently in cooking. It is inexpensive and easy to obtain at a good off-licence, but if you do not have any, use dry sherry instead.

✻ Not suitable for freezing.

Chicken Paella

SERVES 4

100 ml (3½ fl oz) olive oil

4 chicken portions

2 cloves garlic, crushed

1 × 198 g (7 oz) can sweet red peppers, drained and sliced

1 large tomato, skinned and chopped

1.2 litres (2 pints) water

½ teaspoon turmeric

salt and black pepper

350 g (12 oz) Valencia or risotto rice

100 g (4 oz) frozen peas

1 × 170 g (6 oz) jar mussels, drained

cleaned and cooked fresh mussels, to garnish (optional)

Heat the oil in a paella pan or large frying pan. Add the chicken portions and fry over moderate heat for 5 minutes until lightly coloured on all sides.

Add the garlic, red peppers and chopped tomato and continue frying, stirring constantly, for 5 minutes.

Pour in 1 litre (1¾ pints) of the water and add the turmeric and salt and pepper to taste. Bring slowly to the boil, then simmer for 15 minutes.

Add the rice to the pan and stir gently to mix with the other ingredients. Simmer for 10 minutes, stirring frequently, then add the frozen peas and simmer for a further 5 minutes or until both rice and peas are tender. Stir frequently during this time to prevent the rice sticking, and add the remaining water as and when the paella looks dry. Finally, stir in the mussels and heat through.

Taste and adjust seasoning before serving garnished with the mussels if using.

Note: The quantity of olive oil may seem large for British tastes, but it does give the finished dish an authentic Spanish flavour. If you prefer not to use so much, then decrease the quantity – the paella will still taste good.

Serving suggestion: Paella is an easy dish to cook and serve for an informal supper party. If you have a paella pan for serving, it looks really good with its garnish of mussels. Serve with a robust red Spanish wine such as Rioja, and plenty of fresh bread. Follow with a salad of shredded lettuce, green pepper strips, black or green olives and thinly sliced onion, tossed in an olive oil and vinegar dressing.

✳ Not suitable for freezing.

Above Chicken paella, garnished with fresh mussels

Above Chicken and vegetable pie served with sliced courgettes and mint

36

corn, parsley, mustard powder and salt and pepper to taste. Fold in the leeks and chicken, turn into a 1.2 litre (2 pint) pie dish and leave to cool.

Roll out the pastry on a floured surface to make a lid for the pie dish, and roll out a strip to go round the rim of the dish. Brush the rim with water and press on the strip; then brush the strip with water and place the lid on top. Crimp the edges and decorate with pastry trimmings and brush with beaten egg to glaze. Make a hole in the centre of the lid for the steam to escape. Bake for 30 minutes or until golden. Serve hot.

✳ Freeze the pie, before glazing and baking, for up to 3 months. Bake from frozen, covering the pie with foil; allow an extra 20 minutes cooking time.

≈ For microwave cooking, freeze the pie without the pastry crust. Microwave the pie filling on DE-FROST for 10 minutes to thaw, stirring once. Cover and cook on HIGH for 2 minutes. Cover the pie with the pastry crust. Cook on HIGH for 8–9 minutes, until the pastry is well risen and holding its shape, turning frequently. Brown under a preheated hot grill.

Chicken and Vegetable Pie

SERVES 4–6

4 leeks, trimmed and sliced
salt and black pepper
4 cooked chicken portions
50 g (2 oz) butter or margarine
50 g (2 oz) plain flour
300 ml (½ pint) milk
1 × 198 g (7 oz) can sweetcorn, drained
4 tablespoons chopped fresh parsley
½ teaspoon mustard powder
1 × 368 g (13 oz) packet frozen puff pastry, thawed
beaten egg, to glaze

Oven temperature: 200°C (400°F), Gas Mark 6
Blanch the leeks in boiling salted water for 5 minutes. Drain thoroughly, reserving 300 ml (½ pint) of the water. Remove the chicken meat from the bones, discarding the skin, and cut into bite-sized pieces.

Melt the butter or margarine in a saucepan, add the flour and cook, stirring, for 1–2 minutes. Remove from the heat and blend in the reserved blanching liquid and the milk, a little at a time. Bring to the boil, stirring, then simmer for 3 minutes until thick and smooth. Remove from the heat and add the sweet-

Chicken Kebabs with Peanut Sauce

SERVES 4

4 boneless chicken breasts, each about 150 g (5 oz)
finely grated rind and juice of 1 lime or lemon
2 tablespoons olive oil
black pepper
PEANUT SAUCE: 6 tablespoons crunchy peanut butter 3 tablespoons olive oil 2 tablespoons soy sauce juice of 1 lime or lemon 25 g (1 oz) creamed coconut, grated ½ teaspoon chilli powder 300 ml (½ pint) water

Skin the chicken breasts then cut into chunky pieces. Place in a bowl, add the lime or lemon rind and juice, olive oil and pepper to taste. Stir to mix; cover and leave to marinate for 1–4 hours, or overnight.

When ready to serve, prepare the peanut sauce. Put the peanut butter in a saucepan and blend in the remaining ingredients, adding water gradually.

Thread the chicken on to oiled kebab skewers, then cook under a preheated moderate grill for 15–20 minutes, turning frequently.

Meanwhile, bring the sauce slowly to the boil then lower the heat and simmer, stirring frequently, for about 10 minutes until thickened. Pour into a warmed jug or sauceboat and serve hot with the kebabs.

✳ Not suitable for freezing.

Barbecued Roast Chicken

SERVES 4

4 tablespoons Worcestershire sauce

4 tablespoons wine vinegar

4 tablespoons tomato ketchup

4 tablespoons soft dark brown sugar

1 teaspoon chilli powder

1 teaspoon garlic salt

1.5–1.75 kg (3½–4 lb) oven-ready chicken

25 g (1 oz) butter

salt and black pepper

fresh chervil, to garnish

Oven temperature: 200°C (400°F), Gas Mark 6

Put the Worcestershire sauce, vinegar, ketchup and sugar into a bowl. Add the chilli powder and garlic salt and stir well to mix.

Put the chicken into a roasting pan. Melt the butter and brush all over the chicken, then sprinkle with salt and pepper. Roast for 30 minutes.

Remove the chicken from the oven and brush all over with the barbecue sauce. Return to the oven and continue roasting for 1½ hours. Baste the chicken frequently with the pan juices until the skin is a rich dark brown. Serve hot, garnished with fresh chervil.

Serving suggestion: Serve as an unusual alternative to the Sunday roast, with jacket-baked potatoes and seasonal vegetables. Or, serve the chicken Chinese-style with boiled rice or egg noodles and a dish of stir-fried beansprouts, peppers and cucumber – you can add a few tablespoons of the barbecue sauce from the roasting pan to add flavour.

✳ Not suitable for freezing.

Left Barbecued roast chicken, served with an endive and cucumber salad

37

Right Monkfish, scampi and lime brochettes

Turkey Tetrazzini

SERVES 4

75 g (3 oz) butter or margarine
350 g (12 oz) turkey fillet, cut into bite-sized pieces
175 g (6 oz) button mushrooms, sliced
175 g (6 oz) spaghetti
salt and black pepper
65 g (2½ oz) plain flour
750 ml (1¼ pints) milk
100 g (4 oz) Gruyère cheese, grated
4 tablespoons dry sherry
¼ teaspoon ground mace
2 tablespoons grated Parmesan cheese

Oven temperature: 180°C (350°F), Gas Mark 4

Melt half of the butter or margarine in a saucepan, add the turkey and cook for about 10 minutes until lightly coloured and just tender. Remove with a slotted spoon and set aside.

Add the mushrooms to the pan and cook for a few minutes until softened. Remove with a slotted spoon and set aside with the turkey.

Cook the spaghetti in a large pan of boiling salted water for 12–15 minutes until tender.

Meanwhile, make the cheese sauce. Melt the remaining butter in the pan in which the turkey and mushrooms were cooked. Add the flour and cook, stirring, for 1–2 minutes. Blend in the milk a little at a time. Bring to the boil, stirring, then simmer for 3 minutes until thick and smooth. Add the Gruyère cheese, sherry, mace and salt and pepper to taste and continue simmering and stirring until the cheese has melted. Remove from the heat.

Drain the spaghetti, return to the pan and add about half of the cheese sauce. Stir well to mix, then arrange around the edge of a buttered ovenproof dish.

Stir the turkey and mushrooms into the remaining cheese sauce and pour into the centre of the dish. Sprinkle with the Parmesan and bake for 20 minutes until golden. Serve hot.

Note: Tetrazzini is an American dish, believed to have been invented by emigré Italians, hence the Italian-sounding name. Chicken is often used instead of turkey.

Serving suggestion: A filling family supper dish which children love, Turkey tetrazzini needs only a simple green or tomato salad to accompany it.

✻ Not suitable for freezing.

of fish, 2 scampi, 2 bacon rashers and 1 bay leaf on each skewer. Brush with any marinade left in the bowl.

Grill under a preheated moderate grill for 8–10 minutes, turning frequently. Serve immediately, with lime wedges.

Note: Monkfish (sometimes also called angler fish) is excellent for pies and kebabs because it has a very thick, dense texture and so does not fall apart easily during cooking as other white fish tend to do. Monkfish has a flavour similar to lobster, yet is far less expensive, and is used a lot in Mediterranean cuisines – the French call it *lotte*, the Spanish *rape* and the Italians *rospo*. Most good fishmongers stock monkfish, or you can order it in advance.

Serving suggestion: Serve for a special light main course on a bed of boiled rice, followed by a lettuce, watercress and cucumber salad and French bread. Chilled dry white wine is the ideal drink to serve.

Variation: Cooked and shelled mussels can be used instead of the scampi or prawns.

✳ Not suitable for freezing.

Monkfish, Scampi and Lime Brochettes

SERVES 4

1 kg (2 lb) monkfish fillets
6 tablespoons olive oil
4 tablespoons lime or lemon juice
2 tablespoons crushed green peppercorns
salt and black pepper
16 streaky bacon rashers, rinded
16 peeled scampi or large prawns
8 bay leaves
lime wedges, to serve

Skin the monkfish and cut into 24 chunks. Put the oil and lime or lemon juice in a bowl with the pepper-corns and salt and pepper to taste. Whisk until well combined, then add the chunks of monkfish and fold gently until coated in the marinade. Cover and leave to marinate in the refrigerator for 1–4 hours.

Cut each bacon rasher across in half, then roll each half up. Thread the cubes of monkfish on 8 oiled kebab skewers, alternating them with the scampi, bacon rolls and bay leaves, so that there are 3 cubes

Mackerel with Shallot and Parsley Stuffing

SERVES 6

4 mackerel, each about 275–350 g (10–12 oz) cleaned, heads and tails removed
4 tablespoons lemon juice
lemon wedges, to garnish

STUFFING:
50 g (2 oz) butter
2 shallots, finely chopped
4 tablespoons chopped fresh parsley
75 g (3 oz) fresh wholemeal breadcrumbs
1 teaspoon finely grated lemon rind
1–2 tablespoons dry white wine
salt and black pepper

First make the stuffing. Heat the butter in a saucepan, add the shallots and fry until soft and lightly coloured. Add the parsley, breadcrumbs and lemon rind. Stir well and mix in enough wine to bind. Season well. Use the mixture to stuff each mackerel.

Make 3 diagonal cuts on each side of the fish, and sprinkle each one with the lemon juice.

Grill the mackerel under a preheated hot grill for 2–3 minutes on each side. Lower the heat to moderate and cook for a further 5 minutes on each side or until cooked through. Serve garnished with lemon wedges.

Variation: Use herrings instead of the mackerel and reduce the stuffing by one-third.

✳ Not suitable for freezing.

CLEANING A MACKEREL

Cover the chopping board with a few sheets of greaseproof paper. Holding the fish by the tail, scrape off the scales with a heavy blunt knife, working towards the head of the fish.

Using a sharp knife, cut open the belly of the fish from the gills to the tail. Scrape out the entrails and rinse the fish under cold running water. Pat dry with kitchen paper.

39

Above Sole Florentine, garnished with lemon slices

Ginger Seafood Platter

SERVES 4

about 350 g (12 oz) thick, firm-fleshed white fish fillets

1 kg (2 lb) mussels, cooked, shelled and dried

450 g (1 lb) frozen shelled scallops, thawed

4 large (Dublin Bay or Mediterranean) prawns

2 tablespoons plain flour

2 teaspoons ground ginger

salt and black pepper

vegetable oil, for deep frying

lemon wedges, to serve

BATTER:
225 g (8 oz) plain flour
4 tablespoons maize flour
4 tablespoons arrowroot
1 × 330 ml (11.6 fl oz) can ginger beer

Oven temperature: 150°C (300°F), Gas Mark 2
First make the batter. Sift the flours and arrowroot into a bowl with a pinch of salt. Add the ginger beer, whisking vigorously until a smooth batter is formed. Set aside while preparing the fish.

Skin the white fish and cut into large chunks. Thread the mussels on oiled wooden cocktail sticks, allowing 3–4 per stick. Dry the scallops thoroughly with kitchen paper. Peel the prawns.

Spread the flour out on a plate and mix in the ginger with salt and pepper to taste. Add the fish and seafood and coat in the flour mixture.

Heat the oil in a deep-fat fryer to 190°C (375°F) or until a cube of stale bread browns in 30 seconds. Keep the cooked food warm while frying in batches.

Dip a batch of the fish and seafood in the batter. Lift out individual pieces with a slotted spoon and lower into the hot oil. Deep-fry for 4–5 minutes until crisp and light golden. Remove with a clean slotted spoon and discard the cocktail sticks. Drain quickly on kitchen paper. Serve immediately, with lemon wedges.

Note: The batter for the fish is light and delicate, not the usual heavy kind of batter normally used for deep-frying fish. To be enjoyed at its best it should be eaten immediately after frying each batch, but if you and your guests all want to eat together, it will keep for a short while in a hot oven.

Variation: The mixture of fish and seafood suggested here gives a good balance of textures and colours, but you can use whatever you like. The large prawns are an expensive luxury, but well worth it if you are entertaining.

✳ Not suitable for freezing.

Sole Florentine

SERVES 4

75 g (3 oz) butter, diced

4 small Dover or lemon sole

juice of 2 lemons

750 g (1½ lb) cooked spinach, chopped or 2 × 275 g (10 oz) packets frozen chopped spinach, thawed

2 × 150 g (5.29 oz) cartons natural yogurt

50 g (2 oz) Parmesan cheese, grated

pinch of grated nutmeg

salt and black pepper

lemon slices, to garnish

Grease the base of the grill pan generously with one-third of the butter. Arrange the sole in the pan, sprinkle with half the lemon juice and dot with half the remaining butter. Place under a preheated hot grill for about 10 minutes, turning once and basting frequently with the remaining lemon juice and butter.

Place the spinach in a saucepan with the yogurt, half the Parmesan and the nutmeg and heat gently, stirring continuously. (Do not boil or the yogurt will curdle.) Season to taste.

Place the spinach mixture on a large heated serving dish and arrange the grilled fish on top. Sprinkle the remaining cheese over the fish and place under the grill until browned. Garnish with lemon slices.

✳ Not suitable for freezing.

Salmon Steaks with Dill Butter Sauce

SERVES 6

6 salmon steaks, each weighing about 100 g (4 oz)

STOCK:
150 ml (¼ pint) dry white wine
150 ml (¼ pint) fish stock
few sprigs parsley
1 bay leaf
1 small onion, quartered

SAUCE:
150 ml (¼ pint) fish stock
150 g (5 oz) butter
1 teaspoon flour
1 tablespoon double cream
1 tablespoon chopped fresh dill or 2 teaspoons dried dill
salt and black pepper

sprigs of fresh dill, to garnish

Oven temperature: 180°C (350°F), Gas Mark 4

Boil the stock ingredients together for 15 minutes.

Lay the salmon steaks in a shallow baking dish. Pour the stock over the fish and cover tightly with foil. Bake for 5–10 minutes or until cooked but just firm. Lift out carefully with a fish slice and transfer to a warmed serving dish. Keep warm. Strain and reserve the cooking liquid.

To make the sauce, add the reserved cooking liquid to the fish stock to make it 300 ml (½ pint). Melt 25 g (1 oz) of the butter in a small saucepan and gradually stir in the flour. Add the stock and stir until boiling.

Cut the remaining butter into small dice and whisk it, one piece at a time, into the boiling sauce. Lower the heat then add the cream and dill. Stir constantly until the sauce thickens and becomes creamy. Season to taste and pour around the fish. Serve immediately garnished with sprigs of fresh dill.

Serving suggestion: Lightly steamed leeks or green beans would go well with this dish.

✻ Freeze for up to 1 month. To thaw and heat, put in an ovenproof dish, cover with foil and bake from frozen in a 190°C (375°F), Gas Mark 5 oven for 25 – 35 minutes.

Left Salmon steaks with dill butter sauce

41

Pheasant with Wine and Juniper Berries

SERVES 4–6

100 g (4 oz) streaky bacon rashers, rinded and chopped

1 small onion, finely chopped

2 oven-ready pheasants

4 tablespoons brandy

300 ml (½ pint) full-bodied red wine

finely grated rind and juice of 1 orange

2 tablespoons juniper berries, crushed

2 bay leaves

1 teaspoon dried mixed herbs

salt and black pepper

TO GARNISH:
1 orange, peeled and sliced
fresh parsley sprigs

Oven temperature: 180°C (350°F), Gas Mark 4

Put the bacon in a frying pan and fry over moderate heat until the fat runs. Add the onion and fry until soft and lightly coloured.

Add the pheasants one at a time and fry until browned on all sides, then transfer to a large flameproof casserole dish. Warm the brandy in a separate small pan, ignite and pour over the pheasants

When the flames die down, pour in the wine, add the orange rind and juice and bring to the boil. Remove from the heat; add the remaining ingredients. Cover and bake for 45–60 minutes or until tender.

Remove the pheasants from the cooking liquid and keep warm on a serving platter. Discard the bay leaves. Transfer the casserole to the hob. Boil rapidly, stirring, for a few minutes to reduce slightly then taste and adjust seasoning.

Garnish the pheasants with orange slices and parsley. Serve hot, with the sauce handed separately in a warmed sauceboat.

Note: Fresh pheasants are in season from 1 October to 31 January; but frozen pheasants are available all year round from most butchers and large supermarkets. If using frozen birds, thaw for 24 hours in the refrigerator before cooking.

✳ Cool the pheasants after cooking in the oven. Freeze for up to 3 months. Thaw in the refrigerator overnight, then reheat until bubbling on the hob for about 20 minutes, and continue with the recipe as above.

≈ Microwave on DEFROST for 10–12 minutes. Leave to stand for 10–15 minutes, then continue with the recipe as above.

Rabbit in Mustard Sauce

SERVES 4

4 rabbit legs, thawed and thoroughly dried if frozen

3 tablespoons plain flour

salt and black pepper

3 tablespoons oil

1 large onion, finely chopped

440 ml (¾ pint) can lager

2 tablespoons green peppercorn mustard

2 teaspoons dried rosemary

TO GARNISH:
1–2 tablespoons green peppercorns
lime or lemon slices

Coat each rabbit leg in the flour seasoned with salt and pepper. Shake off and reserve the excess flour.

Heat the oil in a large flameproof casserole, add the rabbit and fry over moderate heat until lightly browned on all sides. Remove and set aside.

Add the onion to the pan and fry gently until soft and lightly coloured. Sprinkle in the reserved flour and cook for 1–2 minutes, stirring all the time. Pour in the lager and bring to the boil, stirring constantly. Add the mustard and rosemary. Lower the heat and return the rabbit to the pan. Cover and simmer gently for 45 minutes or until the rabbit is tender.

Taste and adjust the seasoning of the sauce. Cover the base of a warmed serving platter with a pool of the sauce, then place the rabbit pieces on top. Pour more sauce carefully over the rabbit and garnish with peppercorns and lime or lemon slices. Serve hot, with any remaining sauce handed separately.

Note: Mild green peppercorn mustard and green peppercorns are now widely available from large supermarkets and Continental delicatessens. You can use any French mustard (such as Dijon), although you may want to decrease the quantity slightly as it is stronger.

Serving suggestion: Lager and green peppercorns transform humble rabbit portions into an unusual and special dish – ideal for a family treat midweek or at the weekend. Serve with creamed potatoes or boiled rice and buttered matchstick carrots tossed with chopped fresh herbs and black pepper.

✳ Freeze for up to 3 months. Thaw at room temperature for about 4 hours before reheating on the hob for about 20 minutes.

≈ Microwave on DEFROST for 20 minutes to thaw. Allow to stand for 5 minutes. Microwave on HIGH for 8–10 minutes to reheat, stirring twice.

Opposite: Top Rabbit in mustard sauce; **Bottom** Pheasant with wine and juniper berries, served with brown rice and parsley

Baked Potatoes with Thyme Butter

SERVES 4

4 old potatoes, each weighing about 225 g (8 oz)

8 rashers streaky bacon

100 g (4 oz) butter, softened

2 tablespoons finely chopped fresh thyme

4 tablespoons single cream or milk

salt and black pepper

Oven temperature: 200°C (400°F), Gas Mark 6
Scrub the potatoes and prick the skins all over with a fork. Place on the open shelf of the oven; bake for 1–1½ hours or until they are soft when squeezed.

While the potatoes are baking, roll up the bacon rashers and secure each with a cocktail stick. Place on a baking tray and bake for 10 minutes or until crisp and brown. Remove the cocktail sticks when cooked.

Blend the butter with the thyme. Roll into a cylinder shape; wrap in greaseproof paper and chill.

Cut a slice from the top of each baked potato, scoop out the flesh and mash with the cream or milk and season with salt and pepper. Pile back into the skins and return to the oven for 10–15 minutes or until very hot. Top each potato with two bacon rolls and a slice of thyme butter. Serve immediately.

✳ Freeze the filled potatoes for up to 3 months. Reheat straight from the freezer at 200°C (400°F), Gas Mark 6 for 40 minutes. Top with thyme butter when hot. The thyme butter will also freeze for 3 months. Thaw in the refrigerator for 4 hours. Prepare the bacon rolls while reheating the potatoes.

Below Baked potatoes with thyme butter

Spinach Roulade

SERVES 6–8

275 g (10 oz) frozen chopped spinach, thawed

¼ teaspoon salt

¼ teaspoon ground mace

25 g (1 oz) flour

25 g (1 oz) butter

150 ml (¼ pint) milk

3 eggs, separated

50 g (2 oz) Parmesan cheese, grated

90 g (3½ oz) jar lumpfish roe, to serve

FILLING:
150 g (5 oz) cream cheese
few drops of lemon juice
1 × 142 ml (5 fl oz) carton whipping cream, whipped

Oven temperature: 190°C (375°F), Gas Mark 5
Grease a Swiss roll tin 30 × 23 cm (12 × 9 inch) and line with greaseproof paper. Grease and dust the paper with flour. Have ready a separate sheet of greaseproof paper dusted with flour.

Cook the spinach with the salt and mace in a saucepan over low heat. Do not add any liquid. Add the flour and butter and stir well. Stir in the milk and cook until thick. Beat in the egg yolks and cheese.

Whisk the egg whites stiffly and fold into the cooked mixture. Turn into the prepared tin and bake for about 20 minutes or until set and lightly browned. Turn out on to the prepared greaseproof paper. Cool slightly then carefully peel off the baking paper. Roll up with the floured paper.

To make the filling, put the cream cheese and lemon juice in a bowl and beat until creamy. Fold in the whipped cream. Carefully unroll the roulade and remove paper. Spread with the filling and roll up. Cut into slices and serve with the lumpfish roe.

✳ Freeze the roulade, rolled with the floured paper and before filling. Store for up to 1 month. Thaw at room temperature for 1 hour. Unroll and fill.

≋ Microwave on DEFROST for 2–3 minutes. Allow to stand for 5–10 minutes. Unroll and fill.

Braised Red Cabbage with Chestnuts

SERVES 6–8

1 tablespoon olive oil
100 g (4 oz) streaky bacon rashers
2 large onions, halved and thinly sliced
1 kg (2 lb) red cabbage, cut into 1 cm (½ inch) slices
4 carrots, cut into thin strips
450 g (1 lb) Bramley or other tart cooking apples, peeled, cored and roughly chopped
2 garlic cloves, finely crushed
pinch of ground cloves
pinch of grated nutmeg
salt and black pepper
1 bouquet garni
150 ml (¼ pint) dry red wine
1 × 285 g (9.8 oz) can chestnuts, drained and quartered

Oven temperature: 160°C (325°F), Gas Mark 3

Heat the oil in a frying pan. Rind and chop the bacon and add with the onions. Fry gently for 5 minutes without browning.

Arrange the cabbage, bacon and onions, carrots, apples and garlic, in layers in a deep ovenproof dish, seasoning each layer with cloves, nutmeg and salt and pepper to taste. Put the bouquet garni in the centre of the casserole, then pour over the wine.

Cover and bake for 1 hour. Remove from the oven and stir in the chestnuts, cover and return to the oven for a further 1–1½ hours or until the vegetables are tender. Remove the bouquet garni before serving.

Serving suggestion: Serve with roast chicken, pheasant or pork.

✳ Freeze for up to 3 months. Thaw overnight in the refrigerator. To serve, reheat gently to boiling point then simmer for 2–3 minutes.

≋ Microwave on HIGH for 12 minutes, stirring twice, to thaw and reheat.

Left Braised red cabbage with chestnuts; **Right** Spinach roulade

Broad Beans with Red Peppers

SERVES 6

450 g (1 lb) frozen broad beans

1 small red pepper, cored, seeded and diced

SAUCE:
2 tablespoons flour
400 ml (14 fl oz) milk
salt and black pepper
squeeze of lemon juice
75 g (3 oz) unsalted butter, cut in small cubes

First make the sauce. Put the flour into a bowl and gradually whisk in the milk. Set the bowl over a saucepan of barely simmering water. Cook over moderate heat, stirring occasionally, for 30 minutes until the sauce is thick and smooth. Season to taste with salt, pepper, and lemon juice.

Remove the pan from the heat and beat in the butter, one cube at a time.

Meanwhile, cook the beans in boiling water. Add the pepper for the last 5 minutes. Drain the beans, then pour over the sauce. Arrange in a warmed serving dish and serve while hot.

Note: The sauce may be cooled, covered and stored in the refrigerator for up to 24 hours.

Serving suggestion: Serve with vegetable burgers as part of a vegetarian meal.

✱ Put the sauce (before adding the butter) into small pots, cover and store in the freezer for up to 1 month. Thaw at room temperature for about 1 hour. Reheat over hot water then beat in the butter as directed.

Swiss Potato Layer

SERVES 6

1 kg (2 lb) floury potatoes, peeled and thinly sliced

40 g (1½ oz) butter

2 cloves garlic, halved

300 ml (½ pint) milk

1 × 142 ml (5 fl oz) carton single cream

pinch of grated nutmeg

salt and black pepper

100 g (4 oz) Emmenthal or Gruyère cheese, grated

Oven temperature: 180°C (350°F); then: 200°C (400°F), Gas Mark 4; then: Gas Mark 6

Lightly grease a shallow casserole dish and cover the base with potato slices, overlapping, to a depth of about 2.5–4 cm (1–1½ inches).

Melt the butter in a pan, add the garlic and fry until golden brown. Remove and discard the garlic and pour the garlic-flavoured butter over the potatoes.

Meanwhile, heat the milk and cream in a saucepan without allowing to boil. Season with the nutmeg, and salt and pepper to taste and pour over the potatoes. Cover the dish with foil and bake for about 40 minutes.

Remove the foil and sprinkle with the grated cheese. Increase the oven temperature to 200°C (400°F) and bake for a further 20 minutes, uncovered, until the top is crisp and golden. Serve immediately.

Serving suggestion: Serve with assorted cold meats and salad.

Variation: Use Cheddar or Edam cheese instead of the Emmenthal or Gruyère.

✳ Freeze for up to 4 months. Thaw at room temperature for 2–3 hours. Bake in a 200°C (400°F), Gas Mark 6 oven for 30 minutes.

≈ Cover and cook on DEFROST for 12 minutes to thaw. Allow to stand for 10 minutes. Cook on HIGH for 4–6 minutes to reheat.

Sweet and Sour Beetroot

SERVES 4

500 g (1¼ lb) small raw beetroots
2 tablespoons cornflour
3 tablespoons sugar
2 tablespoons cold water
1 tablespoon lemon juice
about 100 ml (3½ fl oz) red wine
salt and black pepper

TOPPING:
2 teaspoons polyunsaturated margarine
25 g (1 oz) brown breadcrumbs

Scrub the beets and cook in a large saucepan of boiling salted water over moderate heat for 40–50 minutes. Test by rubbing the back of a fork over a beet; the skin should rub off easily. Drain and leave to cool. Reserve the cooking liquid.

Cut off the tops and tails of the beets and pull off the skins. Cut the beets into thick slices and place in a serving dish.

To make the topping, heat the margarine in a small frying pan over moderate heat until it begins to brown. Stir in the crumbs and fry until golden brown.

Blend together the cornflour and sugar with the cold water. Put 200 ml (7 fl oz) of the reserved beetroot cooking liquid into a saucepan and bring to the simmer. Stir into the cornflour mixture. Return to the saucepan and cook, stirring constantly, for 2–3 minutes until thick and smooth.

Stir in the lemon juice, and enough wine to give a smooth pouring consistency. Season to taste with salt and pepper. Spoon the sauce over the beets and sprinkle over the topping. Serve immediately.

Note: The beets in their sauce may be prepared several hours in advance. Cool, cover, and store in the refrigerator. Reheat in a 190°C (375°F), Gas Mark 5 oven for 10–15 minutes. Prepare the crumbs in advance, too, and add at the last minute.

Variations: Use ready-cooked beetroots if preferred. Make the sauce with 200 ml (7 fl oz) of vegetable or chicken stock.

✳ Not suitable for freezing.

Opposite: Left Broad beans with red peppers; **Centre** Swiss potato layer; **Right** Sweet and sour beetroot

47

Parsnip Moulds with Tomato Sauce

SERVES 3–6

500 g (1¼ lb) parsnips, peeled and cut in thick slices

1 tablespoon soft vegetable margarine

1 tablespoon flour

150 ml (¼ pint) milk

2 eggs

¼ teaspoon ground mace

¼ teaspoon curry powder

salt

coriander sprigs, to garnish

TOMATO SAUCE:
100 g (4 oz) onions, chopped
450 g (1 lb) tomatoes, quartered
sprig of parsley
1 teaspoon salt
¼ teaspoon sugar

COOKING PARSNIP MOULDS

Stand the moulds in a shallow water bath or *bain marie* which has been preheated in the oven.

Oven temperature: 150°C (300°F), Gas Mark 2
Cook the parsnips in a saucepan of boiling salted water for 10–12 minutes or until tender. Reserve 2–3 pieces and drain and mash the remainder.

Grease 6 individual moulds. Half fill a roasting pan with water and heat in the oven.

Melt the margarine in a small saucepan over low heat and stir in the flour. Gradually stir in the milk and cook until thick and smooth. Beat into the mashed parsnips then beat in the eggs. Season with the mace, curry powder, and salt to taste.

Divide the mixture among the moulds. Put the moulds into the pan of water. Bake for 25–30 minutes until set. Test by inserting a sharp knife into the centre, if it comes out clean the moulds are done.

Meanwhile, make the tomato sauce. Put all the ingredients into a saucepan. Cover and cook over low heat for 30–40 minutes, stirring occasionally, until thick. Sieve or place in a blender or food processor until smooth. Return to the pan and keep hot.

To serve, loosen the moulds around the sides with a knife and turn out on to a hot serving dish. Cut the reserved parsnips into strips and lay a few strips on each mould. Spoon the sauce around and serve immediately, garnished with coriander sprigs.

Note: The uncooked moulds may be prepared several hours in advance and stored in the refrigerator ready for cooking when required.

✳ The sauce may be frozen for up to 6 months. To serve, reheat gently from frozen, turning the block frequently to thaw evenly.

≋ Microwave the sauce on HIGH for 5–6 minutes, stirring twice, to thaw and reheat.

Stuffed Aubergine

SERVES 4

4 tablespoons oil

75 g (3 oz) onion, chopped

2 aubergines, each about 350 g (12 oz)

175 g (6 oz) button mushrooms, sliced

1 tablespoon lemon juice

grated rind of 1 lemon

1 teaspoon dried rosemary

4 medium tomatoes, skinned and diced

200 g (7 oz) Mozzarella cheese

salt and black pepper

Oven temperature: 180°C (350°F), Gas Mark 4
Heat the oil in a large frying pan over low heat. Add the onion and cook, stirring occasionally, for about 10 minutes or until translucent.

Cut the aubergines in half lengthways. Using a grapefruit knife, cut out the flesh. Cut the flesh into cubes and add to the pan with the mushrooms. Stir and cook for about 10 minutes until the vegetables are tender. Stir in the lemon juice and rind, and the rosemary. Remove from the heat.

Add the tomatoes and stir gently. Dice all but 50 g (2 oz) of the cheese and stir in lightly with salt and pepper to taste. Pile the mixture into the aubergine shells. Put them into a shallow ovenproof dish, cover with foil and bake for 30 minutes.

Remove the foil from the dish. Cut the remaining cheese into matchstick pieces and arrange on top of the aubergines. Return to the oven for 5 minutes to melt the cheese.

Serve immediately.

Serving suggestion: Serve as a light supper dish with a rich home-made tomato sauce and buttered brown rice.

✳ Freeze for up to 4 months. To serve, reheat from frozen in a 160°C (325°F) Gas Mark 3 oven for about 1 hour. Garnish and serve.

≋ Microwave on DEFROST for 10 minutes to thaw. Allow to stand for 10 minutes. Microwave on HIGH for 6–8 minutes, rearranging once.

Bubble and Squeak Bake

SERVES 4

750 g (1½ lb) old potatoes, peeled

salt and black pepper

3 tablespoons milk

25 g (1 oz) butter

450 g (1 lb) cabbage, chopped

1 small onion, finely chopped

75 g (3 oz) Cheddar cheese, grated

Oven temperature: 200°C (400°F), Gas Mark 6

Put the potatoes in a large saucepan. Cover with salted water and boil until soft. Drain and mash with the milk and butter.

Bring another pan of salted water to the boil. Plunge in the cabbage and boil for 5 minutes. Drain well. Combine the potato and cabbage with the chopped onion. Season with salt and pepper.

Spoon into an oiled baking dish and top with the grated cheese. Bake for about 30–40 minutes or until evenly browned.

Serving suggestion: Serve as a vegetable accompaniment to casseroles and stews or on its own for a substantial supper dish.

Variation: Add 50 g (2 oz) grilled bacon, crumbled, with the cheese.

✳ Freeze for up to 3 months. Thaw overnight in the refrigerator. Reheat in a hot oven, 220°C (425°F), Gas Mark 7 for 30 minutes.

Above Parsnip moulds with tomato sauce

Fried Onion Rings with Horseradish Dip

SERVES 4

6 tablespoons plain flour
pinch of salt
1 egg, beaten
150 ml (¼ pint) light ale
oil, for deep frying
2 Spanish onions, sliced and separated into rings

DIP:
1 × 150 g (5.29 oz) carton natural yogurt
1 tablespoon chopped parsley
1 teaspoon horseradish sauce
pinch of sugar

Sift the flour with the salt into a mixing bowl. Make a well in the centre and add the egg. Using a wire whisk, gradually draw the flour into the egg, adding the ale a little at a time. Beat well to make a smooth batter. Leave to stand for about 15 minutes.

Meanwhile, prepare the dip. Place the yogurt in a bowl, add the parsley, horseradish and sugar and beat until thoroughly blended.

Heat the oil in a deep-frying pan to 190°C (375°F) or until a cube of stale bread dropped into the oil browns in 30 seconds. Working in batches, dip the onion rings into the batter, lower into the oil and fry until crisp and golden brown. Drain on kitchen paper and keep warm while cooking the remainder.

Serve the onion rings immediately, with the dip.

✱ Freeze the onion rings for up to 2 months. To serve, put frozen onion rings on a baking sheet and bake at 200°C (400°F), Gas Mark 6 for 15 minutes. The dip is not suitable for freezing.

Melt the butter in a saucepan, add the garlic and fry until brown. Remove and discard the garlic.

Add the mushrooms, tomatoes and fennel to the pan and cook over low heat for 4–5 minutes. Stir in the stock. Season with salt and pepper to taste and simmer gently for about 15 minutes until tender.

Add the tomato purée, mustard, cream and fennel seeds and stir well. Transfer to a warmed dish and serve.

✳ Freeze for up to 3 months. Thaw at room temperature for 2–3 hours. To serve, reheat gently to boiling point then simmer for 2–3 minutes.

≈ Microwave on DEFROST for 10 minutes. Allow to stand for 10 minutes. Microwave on HIGH for 4–6 minutes, stirring twice to reheat.

French Beans with Herb Hollandaise

SERVES 4

350 g (12 oz) small green beans, trimmed

HERB HOLLANDAISE SAUCE:
1 tablespoon snipped chives
1 tablespoon finely chopped onion
1 teaspoon finely chopped rosemary
½ teaspoon green peppercorns
grated rind of ½ lemon
3 tablespoons white wine
1 tablespoon lemon juice
3 egg yolks
100g (4 oz) unsalted butter, softened
4 tablespoons single cream
salt

To make the hollandaise, put the chives, onion, rosemary, peppercorns, lemon rind, wine and lemon juice into a small saucepan. Set over low heat and simmer until the liquid is reduced to about half. Strain into a small bowl.

Add the egg yolks to the bowl and set over a saucepan of hot, not boiling, water. Place the pan over low heat and whisk until the mixture begins to thicken. Whisk in 2 teaspoons of the butter, one teaspoon at a time.

Remove the bowl from the heat. Gradually whisk in the rest of the butter and the cream to make a glossy, smooth sauce which just holds its shape. Add salt.

Put the beans in a saucepan of boiling salted water and cook for about 5 minutes until tender but still crisp and bright green. Drain and arrange on 4 plates. Pour the sauce into 4 small ramekins and serve tepid.

✳ Freeze the sauce for up to 1 month. To thaw, leave in a warm place but not near direct heat for 30–60 minutes. To reheat, pour the sauce into a bowl and set over a pan of warm, not hot, water. Stir frequently until tepid. If the sauce separates at any stage, drop in an ice cube and stir until the sauce becomes creamy again.

51

Left Fennel Provençale; **Right** French beans with herb hollandaise

Fennel Provençale

SERVES 4

25 g (1 oz) butter

3 cloves garlic, halved

200 g (7 oz) mushrooms, sliced

275 g (10 oz) tomatoes, quartered

2 medium-sized heads fennel, quartered

300 ml (½ pint) vegetable stock

salt and black pepper

1 tablespoon tomato purée

1 teaspoon French mustard

1 tablespoon double cream

1 teaspoon fennel seeds

St. Clement's Sweet Potatoes

SERVES 4–6

350 g (12 oz) orange sweet potatoes, peeled and cubed

350 g (12 oz) white sweet potatoes, peeled and cubed

2 tablespoons orange juice

shredded rind of ½ orange

2 tablespoons lemon juice

shredded rind of 1 lemon

50 g (2 oz) butter

3 tablespoons sugar

black pepper

fresh dill sprigs, to garnish

Put the sweet potatoes into 2 separate saucepans of boiling salted water. Cover and cook for about 10 minutes or until tender. Drain and return to the pans.

To the orange potatoes add the orange juice and rind, and to the white potatoes the lemon juice and rind. Add half the butter and half the sugar to each, then mash with a wooden spoon. Stir over a low heat to melt the sugar. Season to taste with black pepper.

Pile the two vegetables side by side in a hot serving dish. Garnish with fresh dill sprigs and serve immediately.

Serving suggestions: Serve with baked ham or turkey.

✻ Not suitable for freezing.

Hot Carrot Salad

SERVES 4

350 g (12 oz) carrots, peeled

2 tablespoons olive oil

1 teaspoon wine vinegar

salt

1 tablespoon chopped fresh basil or
1 teaspoon dried basil

Grate the carrots with a medium grater. Heat the oil in a large saucepan over medium heat. Stir in the carrots. Cook for 3–4 minutes, stirring constantly, until heated through.

Mix in the vinegar, salt to taste and the basil. Serve immediately.

Serving suggestions: This is an excellent accompaniment for white fish or grilled poultry or meat.

✻ Not suitable for freezing.

Cauliflower with Almond Butter

SERVES 4

1 cauliflower, trimmed

75 g (3 oz) butter

50 g (2 oz) almond slivers

salt and black pepper

Put the cauliflower in a saucepan of salted water and boil for about 10 minutes, or until just tender when pierced with a skewer. Drain and keep warm on a serving dish.

Melt the butter in a saucepan and add the almonds and seasoning. Pour the melted butter and almonds over the hot cauliflower and serve.

Serving suggestion: Serve with roast poultry or meat.

✻ Not suitable for freezing.

Greek-Style Artichokes

SERVES 4

4 large globe artichokes

1 litre (1¾ pints) water

juice of 2½ lemons

175 ml (6 fl oz) olive oil

1 clove garlic, crushed

2 small onions, chopped

2 teaspoons flour

2 teaspoons chopped almonds

salt and black pepper

Cut the stems off the artichokes, remove the bottom leaves and trim the tips off the remaining leaves with kitchen scissors. Cut off the tops, then cut each artichoke in half lengthways. Soak the artichokes in 750 ml (1¼ pints) of the water and the juice of 2 lemons.

Meanwhile, heat the olive oil in a frying pan and fry the garlic and onions until lightly browned. Stir in the flour. Add the remaining lemon juice, the almonds, and salt and pepper to taste.

Arrange the artichoke halves, cut sides up in a large heavy frying pan. Sprinkle the artichokes with the onion mixture, and pour the remaining water into the pan. Cover and simmer over low heat for 35–40 minutes or until tender. Serve warm or cold.

Top St Clement's sweet potatoes; **Centre** Cauliflower with almond butter; **Bottom** Hot carrot salad

Lemon Custard Sponge

SERVES 4

50 g (2 oz) butter, softened

100 g (4 oz) caster sugar

grated rind of 1 lemon

2 eggs, separated

3 tablespoons lemon juice

50 g (2 oz) self-raising flour

250 ml (9 fl oz) milk

Oven temperature: 160°C (325°F), Gas Mark 3

Half fill a baking pan with water; place in the oven.

Beat together the butter and sugar until pale. Beat in the lemon rind and egg yolks. Stir in the lemon juice and the flour. Gradually mix in the milk to form a mixture like a thick pancake batter. Whisk the egg whites until stiff and fold into the batter.

Turn into an ungreased 900 ml (1½ pint) pie dish. Put the dish into the pan of hot water and bake for about 45 minutes or until the sponge is firm on top and nicely browned.

Serve immediately.

Note: This pudding when cooked, separates into a lemony custard sauce topped with a light sponge.

✱ Not suitable for freezing.

Right Fresh pineapple meringue

Fresh Pineapple Meringue

SERVES 6

1 pineapple, about 1.25 kg (2½ lb)

5 tablespoons white rum

CUSTARD:
1 × 142 ml (5 fl oz) carton double cream
3 egg yolks
1 tablespoon caster sugar

MERINGUE:
3 egg whites
75 g (3 oz) caster sugar

Oven temperature: 190°C (375°F), Gas Mark 5
Cut the pineapple in half lengthways through the stem. With a sharp knife, cut out the flesh taking care not to pierce the skin. Reserve the shells. Discard the hard core and cut the fruit into small pieces. Put into a bowl and spoon the rum over. Cover and leave for 2–3 hours. Drain off the juices and reserve.

To make the custard, put the cream into a bowl and set over a pan of hot water over low heat. Mix the egg yolks and sugar together in another bowl and stir in the steaming hot cream. Return to the heat. Cook, stirring frequently, for 7–8 minutes or until the custard begins to thicken.

Stir in the reserved juices from the pineapple and cook for a further minute. Remove from the heat and put the bowl into cold water to stop the cooking. Leave to cool.

Spoon the pineapple into the shells. Wrap the leaf ends with foil, and put on to a baking sheet. Spoon the custard over the fruit.

Whisk the egg whites stiffly. Fold in the sugar and whisk again, until the meringue is smooth. Pile on to the filled pineapple shells and bake for 5–7 minutes until nicely browned. Serve immediately.

Note: The pineapple and the custard can be prepared well in advance and left in a cool place. Add the custard to the fruit just before making the meringue.

✳ Not suitable for freezing.

Caramel Amber Cake

MAKES A 20 CM (8 INCH) CAKE

1 tablespoon instant coffee

6 tablespoons milk

6 tablespoons oil

2 eggs, separated

175 g (6 oz) soft brown sugar

175 g (6 oz) plain flour

½ teaspoon salt

2 teaspoons baking powder

4 tablespoons Tia Maria

1 x 284 ml (10 fl oz) carton whipping cream, to finish

CARAMEL:
100 g (4 oz) caster sugar
3 tablespoons water

Oven temperature: 160°C (325°F), Gas Mark 3
Line a baking sheet with greaseproof paper, and brush with oil. Oil the inside of a 1.2 litre (2 pint) mould with a centre tube or ring mould baking tin.

Put the instant coffee into a mixing bowl and stir in the milk to dissolve. Add the oil, egg yolks and sugar. Beat briefly with a wooden spoon to mix well. Sift the flour, salt, and baking powder and stir in well. Whisk the egg whites until stiff and fold in.

Turn the mixture into the prepared tin. Bake for 45 minutes until lightly browned and springy to the touch. Turn out on to a wire rack to cool. Cut the cake across in half and spoon the liqueur, a little at a time, over both halves.

To make the caramel, dissolve the sugar in the water in a small saucepan over low heat. Increase the heat and boil rapidly without stirring for about 10 minutes or until the syrup begins to brown. Remove from the heat as soon as the syrup is golden brown and pour it immediately on to the paper-lined baking sheet. Set aside to cool.

Crack the caramel with a rolling pin. Put the pieces into a plastic bag and crush with the rolling pin.

Put the cream in a bowl and whip until it forms soft peaks. Spread a generous layer on the bottom cake and set the top in place. Coat the outside of the cake with the rest of the cream. Sprinkle crushed caramel over the whole surface.

Serving suggestions: Serve with coffee or as a dessert.

✳ Open freeze until firm then pack in a rigid container. Freeze for up to 1 month. Thaw at room temperature for 3 hours.

≈ Microwave on DEFROST for 4–6 minutes, checking regularly. Allow to stand for 30 minutes.

MAKING CRUSHED CARAMEL

Pour the caramel on to a baking sheet.

Allow to cool, then crack with a rolling pin.

For finer pieces, put the caramel into a thick polythene bag and crush with a rolling pin.

COOKING CRÊPES

Pour in enough batter to cover the base of a lightly greased frying pan.

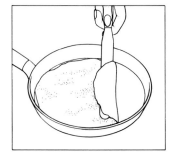

When the top of the crêpe looks opaque, and the underside is cooked, flip the crêpe over and straighten with a palette knife. Allow the second side to brown.

Layer between sheets of greaseproof paper and keep warm.

Opposite Crêpes Suzette

Crêpes Suzette

SERVES 6

100 g (4 oz) plain flour
25 g (1 oz) caster sugar
2 eggs
about 275 ml (9 fl oz) milk
25 g (1 oz) butter, melted
5 tablespoons Cointreau

SAUCE:
4 large sugar cubes
2 large oranges
250 ml (8 fl oz) orange juice
grated rind of 1 orange
50 g (2 oz) butter
50 g (2 oz) caster sugar

Oven temperature: 190°C (375°F), Gas Mark 5

Mix the flour and sugar together in a bowl. Put the eggs and milk into a jug and beat will to mix. Gradually stir into the flour to make a smooth batter. The consistency should be like that of single cream; add 1–2 tablespoons extra milk if necessary.

Brush a 19 cm (7½ inch) omelette pan lightly with butter. Place over moderate heat until hot enough for frying: a drop of batter should cook on the underside almost immediately. Pour in just enough batter to cover the base, tilting the pan to spread evenly. Cook until the underside of the crêpe is golden. Toss or turn and cook on the other side. Repeat, using the remaining batter to make about 12 crêpes.

As the crêpes are cooked, stack them one on top of the other interleaved with greaseproof paper.

To make the sauce, remove the zest from the oranges by rubbing the sugar cubes over the orange skins until they are completely soaked with the orange oil. Put the sugar cubes in a frying pan with the orange juice, orange rind, butter and caster sugar. Stir over moderate heat to dissolve the sugar. Simmer until the mixture begins to thicken into a syrup.

To finish the crêpes, butter a shallow ovenproof dish about 25 × 20 cm (10 × 8 inch). Fold each crêpe in half, then in half again to make fan shapes. Lay in the dish, overlapping neatly. Spoon the orange syrup over, and cover the dish. Place in the oven for 10–15 minutes to heat through.

Put the Cointreau in a small saucepan over moderate heat until it begins to steam. Set alight and pour over the pancakes. Serve immediately with extra orange sauce handed separately in a small jug.

✻ Freeze the crêpes, interleaved with greaseproof paper, for up to 4 months. To serve, separate the crêpes; thaw at room temperature for 30 minutes.

≈ Do not separate the crêpes and microwave on DEFROST for 6 minutes turning twice. Allow to stand for 5 minutes, separate and use as fresh crêpes.

Passion Fruit Pavlova

SERVES 6–8

225 g (8 oz) caster sugar
3 egg whites
½ teaspoon vanilla essence
1 teaspoon white vinegar
1 teaspoon cornflour

TO SERVE:
1 × 284 ml (10 fl oz) carton double or whipping cream
6 passion fruits

Oven temperature: 100°C (200°F), Gas Mark ¼

Brush a baking sheet with oil then line with aluminium foil. Brush with cold water.

Put all the meringue ingredients into a large bowl together. Whisk with an electric mixer for about 8 minutes. The mixture should be very white and stiff.

If you do not have an electric mixer, use a wire whisk or rotary beater. First whisk the egg whites until stiff, then whisk in the remaining ingredients.

Turn out on to the baking sheet. Using a palette knife, smooth the meringue into a round or oblong at least 6 cm (2½ inches) deep.

Bake for 2 hours until set. Turn off the heat and leave the meringue in the oven until cool.

Transfer the meringue to a serving dish. Whip the cream softly and spread all over the meringue. Just before serving, cut the passion fruits in half and scoop out the seeds and pulp. Sprinkle over the surface of the cream.

Serve cut in thick slices.

Note: The finished Pavlova will last for a few hours if stored in the refrigerator.

✻ Not suitable for freezing.

Gooseberry and Hazelnut Layer

SERVES 6

100 g (4 oz) ginger biscuits, crushed
50 g (2 oz) hazelnuts, lightly toasted and chopped
450 g (1 lb) gooseberries
75 g (3 oz) granulated sugar
1 egg white
50 g (2 oz) caster sugar
1 × 284 ml (10 fl oz) carton double cream
6 whole hazelnuts, to decorate

Mix together the biscuit crumbs and hazelnuts and set aside.

Place the gooseberries in a saucepan with the sugar and 4 tablespoons of water. Cover and simmer gently for 15 minutes until tender.

Cool slightly then sieve or place in a blender or food processor and blend until smooth.

Whisk the egg white until stiff, then gradually whisk in the caster sugar, until the mixture forms stiff peaks. Whip the cream until it forms soft peaks. Fold the egg whites then half the cream into the gooseberry purée. Place half the gooseberry mixture in a serving dish followed by a layer of the biscuit and nut mixture. Repeat the layers, finishing with a layer of biscuit and nuts. Pipe the remaining cream around the edge of the dish. Decorate with whole hazelnuts, then chill for several hours before serving.

✳ Freeze for up to 3 months. To serve, thaw in the refrigerator overnight.

≋ Microwave on DEFROST for 5–6 minutes to thaw.

French-style Fruit Tart

SERVES 6

1 × 368 g (13 oz) packet frozen puff pastry, thawed

1 tablespoon flour

1 egg yolk, mixed with 1 teaspoon water

GLAZE:
4 tablespoons apricot jam
2 tablespoons water
1 teaspoon lemon juice

FILLING:
2 kiwi fruits, peeled and sliced
100 g (4 oz) black grapes, seeded
100 g (4 oz) green grapes, seeded
100 g (4 oz) strawberries

Oven temperature: 220°C (425°F), Gas Mark 7
Roll out the pastry to a 23 cm (9 inch) round. Sprinkle the pastry lightly with flour and fold in half.

Cut out a semi-circle from the folded edge, leaving a 3.5 cm (1½ inch) wide band.

Open out the round and roll out to 23 cm (9 inch), to form the base of the tart. Place on a dampened baking sheet, prick all over and dampen the edges.

Open out the band of pastry and place on the base to make a border. Flute the edges and mark a pattern on the border with a knife. Brush the border with the egg yolk and water and bake for 20–25 minutes until golden brown.

To make the glaze, heat the jam with the water and lemon juice then sieve and reheat. Use to brush the base of the pastry case, then arrange the fruit in rows around the tart. Brush the fruit generously with the glaze. Serve cold.

✳ Not suitable for freezing.

Upside-down Apple Flan

SERVES 6

175 g (6 oz) plain flour

100 g (4 oz) butter

1 tablespoon caster sugar

grated rind of 1 small lemon

1 egg yolk

TOPPING:
50 g (2 oz) butter
4 tablespoons caster sugar
750 g (1½ lb) dessert apples
juice of 1 small lemon

Oven temperature: 200°C (400°F), Gas Mark 6

First make the pastry. Sift the flour into a bowl. Rub in the butter with the fingertips until the mixture resembles fine breadcrumbs. Stir in the sugar and lemon rind. Add the egg yolk and bind to form a firm dough. Cover with clingfilm and chill in the refrigerator for 30 minutes.

To make the topping, place the butter in a 20 cm (8 inch) diameter, 5 cm (2 inch) deep cake tin. Melt the butter over a gentle heat, stir in the sugar and continue heating until the sugar begins to brown. Use oven gloves to remove the tin from the heat, and leave to cool.

Peel, core and slice the apples and toss in the lemon juice. Arrange a neat layer of apple slices over the base of the tin. Pack in the remaining apples.

Roll the pastry into a circle the same size as the tin. Carefully place the pastry over the apple slices, press down gently, trim and prick all over with a fork.

Bake for 30 minutes. Cover with foil and continue cooking for a further 25 minutes.

Turn the flan upside-down on to a serving plate. Serve hot or cold.

Serving suggestion: For a special end to a Sunday dinner, serve warm with French vanilla ice cream or fresh whipped cream.

Variations: Substitute the grated rind of a small orange for the lemon in the pastry, and add peeled slices from 2 oranges to the apples in the topping. Mix 2 teaspoons of cinnamon into the caster sugar for the topping. Sprinkle sultanas over the base of the tin before arranging the apple slices, and mix sultanas with the remaining apples before placing the pastry on top.

✳ Freeze for up to 4 months. Thaw at room temperature for 2–3 hours.

≈ Microwave on HIGH for 5 minutes to thaw. Allow to stand for 5 minutes. Cook on HIGH for 2 minutes to reheat.

MAKING AN UPSIDE-DOWN PIE

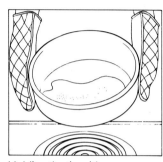

Holding the tin with oven gloves, gently heat the butter and sugar until caramel forms.

Arrange the first layer of apple slices neatly over the caramel.

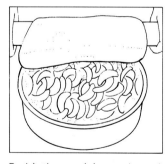

Pack in the remaining apples and place the pastry over, pressing down gently with the fingers.

Rhubarb and Ginger Crumble

SERVES 4–6

750 g (1½ lb) rhubarb

100 g (4 oz) ginger marmalade or preserve

100 g (4 oz) caster sugar

175 g (6 oz) plain flour

½ teaspoon ground ginger

100 g (4 oz) chilled butter or hard margarine, diced

Oven temperature: 200°C (400°F), Gas Mark 6

Cut the rhubarb into 2.5 cm (1 inch) pieces. Put into an ovenproof dish 21 cm diameter × 7.5 cm deep (8½ × 3 inch). Dot the marmalade over the fruit then stir to mix.

Put the sugar, flour, and ginger into a bowl. Add the fat and rub with the fingertips until the mixture resembles fine crumbs. Spread on top of the rhubarb and press flat. Bake for about 30 minutes until browned.

✳ Freeze uncooked for up to 3 months. To serve, bake from frozen in a 220°C (425°F) Gas Mark 7 oven for 20 minutes then at 190°C (375°F) Gas Mark 5 for a further 45 minutes.

≈ Microwave on DEFROST for 10 minutes to thaw. Bake conventionally or microwave on HIGH for 11–13 minutes, turning the dish three times. Brown under a preheated hot grill if liked.

Grilled Nectarines with Ratafia

SERVES 4–6

6 small nectarines

12 tiny ratafia biscuits

4 teaspoons orange liqueur

1 tablespoon caster sugar

1 × 150 g (5.29 oz) carton raspberry yogurt

Make a small cut in the skin of each nectarine. One at a time, place in a small bowl and pour boiling water over. Leave until the skin curls back then remove and hold under cold running water. Pull off the skin.

Cut the fruit in half at the dividing line. Twist the halves apart and prise out the stones with the tip of a knife. Press a biscuit into the cavity of each half.

Arrange the nectarines cut-side up in a shallow flameproof dish about 20 × 15 cm (8 × 6 inches). Drizzle the liqueur over the biscuits then sprinkle sugar over.

Brown under a preheated hot grill for about 3 minutes to caramelize the sugar. Spoon the yogurt on top of the fruit and grill for 1 minute to heat through.

✳ Not suitable for freezing.

Apricot Frangipani

SERVES 4

50 g (2 oz) butter

50 g (2 oz) caster sugar

1 egg

50 g (2 oz) ground almonds

2 tablespoons plain flour

2 tablespoons Amaretto liqueur (optional)

350 g (12 oz) fresh apricots

icing sugar, to dust

Oven temperature: 180°C (350°F), Gas Mark 4

Beat the butter and sugar in a bowl until light and creamy. Beat in the egg, ground almonds, flour, and liqueur until well mixed. Spread into a 20 cm (8 inch) buttered deep flan dish.

Wash the apricots and cut at the dividing line. Twist gently to separate the two halves and release the stones. Press the apricot halves cut-side down into the almond mixture.

Cover the dish with foil and bake for 20 minutes. Remove the foil and bake for a further 20 minutes, or until lightly browned. Dust liberally with icing sugar and serve within a few minutes.

Note: When not in season, substitute canned apricots for fresh; drain, then dry with kitchen paper.

Serving suggestions: Serve with whipped cream or French vanilla ice cream.

✳ Not suitable for freezing.

Left Upside-down apple flan;
Right Apricot frangipani

Pineapple Pecan Slice

SERVES 6

225 g (8 oz) plain flour

75 g (3 oz) caster sugar

100 g (4 oz) butter, cut in small pieces

75 g (3 oz) pecan nuts, finely chopped

1 egg, lightly whisked

FILLING:
350 g (12 oz) can pineapple pieces
50 g (2 oz) caster sugar
3 tablespoons cornflour
2 egg yolks
3 tablespoons Kirsch
1 × 142 ml (5 fl oz) carton double cream

TOPPING:
100 g (4 oz) icing sugar
beaten egg white, to mix
3 pecan nut halves

Oven temperature: 180°C (350°F), Gas Mark 4

To make the pastry, mix the flour and sugar together in a bowl. Add the butter and rub in with the fingertips until the mixture resembles fine crumbs. Stir in the nuts. Add enough of the egg to bind together. Work to a smooth dough. Divide into 4 equal pieces.

Grease 4 baking sheets . Roll each piece of dough 3mm (⅛ inch) thick. With a sharp knife, trim each to a rectangle 25 × 10 cm (10 × 4 inch). Cut one into 6 fingers. Carefully transfer to the baking trays.

Prick the pastry all over with a fork. Bake for about 10 minutes or until the pastry is lightly browned. Slide a palette knife under the pastry to loosen but leave on the sheets to cool.

Meanwhile, make the filling. Reserve 3 pieces of the pineapple then put the remaining pineapple, sugar, cornflour and egg yolks into a saucepan and mix well together. Set over moderate heat and cook, stirring, for 4–5 minutes until well thickened and smooth. Turn into a bowl and stir in the Kirsch. Leave to cool. Whip the cream until soft peaks form and stir in well.

To make the topping, put the icing sugar in a bowl. Gradually stir in the egg white a few drops at a time to make a paste which just barely runs off the back of a spoon.

Lay the fingers of pastry on a wire rack with a piece of greaseproof paper underneath. Carefully spoon topping over each piece to cover completely. Place the nuts and pineapple pieces on alternate fingers. Leave to set for an hour.

To assemble, put one layer of pastry on a serving plate. Spread one-third of the filling over, then carefully set a second piece of pastry on top. Spread with another third of the filling. Lay the third piece of pastry in place, and spread the last of the filling. Lay the iced pastry fingers on top.

Serve within the hour, cut across in slices using a sharp knife.

Serving suggestion: Serve with a scoop of coconut sorbet, garnished with finely chopped orange peel, for a tropical dessert.

Variations: If liked, add a few drops of yellow food colouring to the icing. Substitute mandarin orange slices for the pineapple, and walnuts for the pecans.

✱ Wrap the baked pastry in foil and freeze for up to 1 month. It can be used straight from the freezer as it will thaw by the time the slice is ready for serving.

Coconut-topped Cake

MAKES 15 PIECES

175 g (6 oz) plain flour

1½ teaspoons baking powder

175 g (6 oz) caster sugar

175 g (6 oz) sunflower or soya margarine

3 eggs

2 tablespoons milk

TOPPING:
50 g (2 oz) sunflower or soya margarine
75 g (3 oz) soft brown sugar
100 g (4 oz) desiccated coconut
½ teaspoon vanilla essence
2 tablespoons milk

Oven temperature: 180°C (350°F), Gas Mark 4

Grease and line a cake tin 28 × 18 × 3 cm (11 × 7 × 1¼ inch), with greaseproof paper, letting the paper rise above the tin to form a collar. Grease the inside of the paper.

Put all the cake ingredients into a large bowl and beat until smooth with a wooden spoon or electric mixer. Turn into the prepared tin and smooth the top. Bake for 20–25 minutes or until springy to the touch and lightly browned.

While the cake is baking, prepare the topping. Put all the ingredients into a small saucepan over low heat. Stir until the sugar and fat are melted.

When the cake is baked, lightly spread the topping over the top of the cake. Return to the oven and bake for a further 10 minutes or until lightly browned.

Using the paper collar, carefully lift the cake from the tin. Cool on a wire rack. Serve while fresh, cut in squares or fingers.

✱ Freeze, cut into squares or fingers, for up to 3 months. Thaw on a wire rack at room temperature for 1 hour before serving.

≋ Stand the cakes on kitchen paper. Microwave on HIGH for 1–1¼ minutes, rearranging once. Allow to stand for 5 minutes.

Opposite: Top Pineapple pecan slice; **Bottom** Coconut-topped cake

Orange and Caraway Biscuits

MAKES about 40
50 g (2 oz) caster sugar
100 g (4 oz) plain flour
grated rind of ½ orange
1 teaspoon caraway seeds
50 g (2 oz) butter, diced
1 egg yolk

Oven temperature: 180°C (350°F), Gas Mark 4
Put the sugar, flour, orange rind and caraway seeds into a bowl. Add the butter and rub in until the mixture resembles fine breadcrumbs. Drop in the egg yolk and work with the hand to make a smooth, soft dough. Wrap in foil and chill for about 30 minutes.

Roll the dough out thinly on a lightly floured board. Stamp with a small biscuit cutter. Lift with a palette knife on to greased baking sheets. Bake for 10 minutes or until browned. Cool on wire racks.

Variation: Make the dough into 2 long rolls about 4 cm (1½ inch) in diameter. Wrap in foil and chill for 30–45 minutes. Cut into 3 mm (⅛ inch) slices. Bake as above allowing 2–3 minutes longer.

✳ Freeze, baked or unbaked, for up to 6 months. To serve, thaw cooked biscuits in their container at room temperature for 20 minutes. Unbaked dough should be partly thawed, sliced and baked.

≋ Stand half the baked biscuits on kitchen paper. Microwave on HIGH for 1 minute. Turn over; allow to stand for 10 minutes. Repeat with the remainder.

Banana Teabread

MAKES 18 SLICES
225 g (8 oz) wholewheat flour
170 g (6 oz) caster sugar
2 teaspoons baking powder
40 g (1½ oz) walnuts, finely chopped
450 g (1 lb) ripe bananas, mashed
2 eggs
114 g (4 oz) sunflower margarine, melted

Oven temperature: 150°C (300°F), Gas Mark 2
Grease 1 kg (2 lb) loaf tin. Line with greaseproof paper.

Mix together the flour, sugar, baking powder, and nuts in a large bowl. Make a well in the centre. Put in the bananas, eggs and margarine. Mix briefly but well with a wooden spoon. Turn into the prepared tin. Bake for about 1¼ hours or until cooked in the centre.

Test by inserting a skewer into the teabread. If it comes out clean the teabread is ready.

Remove from the oven and leave for a few minutes. Lift the loaf from the tin by the paper liner. Cool on a wire rack. Wrap in foil or clingfilm and leave in a cool place for a day before cutting.

✳ Freeze for up to 3 months. For convenience, slice and stack interleaved with greaseproof paper, then overwrap the whole loaf. To thaw, the whole loaf will take about 3 hours at room temperature. Individual slices thaw in 30 minutes at room temperature.

≋ Microwave the whole teabread on DEFROST for 6–8 minutes, turning once. Allow to stand for 5–10 minutes. Microwave 1 slice on DEFROST for ½–1 minute.

Swedish Thimble Cookies

MAKES 36
175 g (6 oz) butter, softened
50 g (2 oz) soft brown sugar
1 teaspoon vanilla essence
1 egg yolk
175 g (6 oz) plain flour

TO FINISH:
1 egg white, lightly whisked
75 g (3 oz) hazelnuts, finely chopped
100 g (4 oz) crab-apple jelly

Oven temperature: 180°C (350°F), Gas Mark 4
Put the butter and sugar in a bowl and beat together until light and creamy. Beat in the vanilla essence and the egg yolk. Gradually stir in enough flour to form a soft, smooth dough. Wrap in clingfilm and chill in the refrigerator for 30 minutes.

Divide the mixture into 36 equal pieces and roll into balls. Dip in the egg white then in the nuts. Roll to make an even shape. Place on baking sheets. Press an indentation in the centre of each ball with a thimble or the handle of a small wooden spoon. If the mixture cracks, press together.

Bake for 10–15 minutes until lightly browned and set. Place on wire racks to cool.

Fill with the jelly and serve immediately.

✳ Freeze, baked or unbaked, for up to 6 months. Leave shaped uncooked biscuits on baking sheets at room temperature for 30 minutes before baking. Thaw the dough for about 2 hours at room temperature before shaping and baking. Thaw cooked biscuits for 30 minutes in their container before filling.

≋ Stand baked biscuits on kitchen paper. Microwave on HIGH for 1 minute. Turn over and allow to stand for 10 minutes. Fill as above.

LINING A LOAF TIN

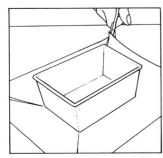

Measure the length and width of the tin and add twice the tin's depth to each of these measurements. Cut a piece of greaseproof paper to this size and position the tin in the centre of the oblong. Make a cut at each corner as shown.

Grease the tin and fold the paper to fit the tin.

Fig Bars

MAKES 20

200 g (7 oz) dried figs

350 ml (12 fl oz) water

2 tablespoons lemon juice

grated rind of 1 lemon

BASE:
200 g (7 oz) butter, diced
300 g (11 oz) plain flour
100 g (4 oz) caster sugar

TOPPING:
50 g (2 oz) caster sugar
2 teaspoons baking powder
2 eggs

Oven temperature: 180°C (350°F), Gas Mark 4
Grease a Swiss roll tin 28 × 18 cm (11 × 7 inch). Line with foil.

First, make the filling. Chop the figs and put with the water, lemon juice, and rind into a saucepan over low heat. Cook gently, stirring frequently, for about 10 minutes to make a thick paste. Set aside to cool.

To make the base, rub the butter finely into the flour and sugar. Press half the mixture firmly into the prepared tin. Spread the fig mixture over the base.

Make the topping by adding the sugar, baking powder and eggs to the remaining base mixture. Mix to a soft dropping consistency; spread over the figs.

Bake for about 45 minutes or until the sponge is lightly brown and feels springy to the touch.

Leave to cool for a few minutes then lift out using the foil lining. Cool on a wire rack. Cut into fingers with a sharp knife. Best served within a day.

✳ Open freeze until firm then pack in a rigid container. Freeze for up to 6 months. Thaw at room temperature for 15 minutes, then serve immediately.

≈ Microwave on DEFROST for 2–3 minutes. Allow to stand for 5 minutes, then serve immediately.

Left Fig bars; **Centre** Orange and caraway biscuits; **Right** Swedish thimble cookies

64

Left Crunchy nut honey buns;
Right Brioche

Brioche

MAKES 12

1 tablespoon caster sugar
2 tablespoons tepid water
2 teaspoons dried yeast
225 g (8 oz) strong white flour
½ teaspoon salt
2 eggs
50 g (2 oz) butter, melted
beaten egg, for glazing

Oven temperature: 190°C (375°F), Gas Mark 5
Dissolve 1 teaspoon of the sugar in the water then sprinkle the yeast over. Leave for about 10 minutes in a warm place until frothy, then stir.

Put the flour, salt and remaining sugar into a large bowl. Add the eggs, butter, and the yeast mixture. Stir vigorously to form a stiff, tacky dough.

Turn out on to a lightly floured surface and knead well for about 10 minutes or until a smooth soft dough is formed. Lightly grease a large bowl. Put the dough in the bowl and cover with clingfilm. Leave in a warm place for 1–1¼ hours or until the dough has doubled in bulk. Turn out on to a well-floured surface and knead briefly.

Grease 12 individual brioche tins. Divide the dough into 12 equal pieces. Cut off about one-third each. Shape the large pieces of dough into smooth balls and set into the prepared tins. Brush with egg. Shape the small pieces of dough into balls and press on top of the larger ones. Press into the centre of each with a well-floured finger. Brush with egg.

Put the tins on to baking sheets and place in large plastic bags. Leave in a warm place for about 45 minutes until well risen. Brush over again with the beaten egg and bake for about 10 minutes or until golden brown.

Serve freshly baked, or cool on wire racks and freeze.

Note: The brioche may be made in the food processor by just putting all the ingredients including the yeast mixture into the processor and working for about 2 minutes or until a ball of dough forms.

✳ Freeze for up to 1 month. To serve, put the frozen brioche on baking sheets and heat in the oven at 180°C (350°F), Gas Mark 4 for about 5 minutes.

≈ Stand on kitchen paper. Microwave on HIGH for 1–1¼ minutes, rearranging once.

Crunchy Nut Honey Buns

MAKES 18

114 g (4 oz) soft margarine

85 g (3 oz) caster sugar

57 g (2 oz) fresh white breadcrumbs

200 ml (7 fl oz) boiling water

2 teaspoons dried yeast

2 tablespoons tepid water

1 egg

370 g (13 oz) wholewheat flour

TOPPING:
85 g (3 oz) clear honey
few chopped almonds

Oven temperature: 190°C (375°F), Gas Mark 5

Put the fat, sugar, and breadcrumbs into a large bowl. Stir in the boiling water until the fat is melted. Allow to cool slightly.

Sprinkle the yeast over the tepid water. Leave in a warm place for about 10 minutes until dissolved and frothy. Then stir. Add the yeast and the egg to the bowl and beat well. Add half the flour and beat again. Stir in the remaining flour to make a stiff but tacky dough.

Scrape down the bowl and cover closely with clingfilm. Place in the refrigerator and leave to rise for 7 hours, or overnight.

Grease 18 deep bun or Yorkshire pudding tins, or use paper baking cases, set on baking sheets.

Scoop out 3 heaped teaspoons of dough, roll into a neat ball and place in a tin or a paper case. When all are filled, cover with large plastic bags and leave in a warm place for 1¼ hours or until the dough has doubled in size.

Put the baking sheets in the oven and bake for about 10 minutes until lightly browned. Brush well with honey, sprinkle a few chopped nuts on top, and return to the oven for 2–3 minutes. Cool on wire racks.

Note: It is important to leave the dough to rise in the refrigerator for at least 7 hours.

Serving suggestions: Spread with butter and jam while fresh. These buns would be an excellent alternative to scones for a tea-time snack; serve with clotted cream and raspberry jam. Serve the warm buns with Lemon, lime and orange curd (page 90).

Variation: Substitute walnuts for the almonds.

✳ Omit the honey and nuts and freeze for up to 1 month. To thaw, place on baking trays and put in the oven at 180°C (350°F), Gas Mark 4 for 3 minutes. Brush with honey, sprinkle with nuts and return to the oven for a further 2 minutes.

Celebration Fruit Cake

SERVES 20–25

175 g (6 oz) dried apricots, soaked and diced

175 g (6 oz) light sultanas

5 tablespoons cold jasmine tea

75 g (3 oz) glacé cherries, quartered

50 g (2 oz) citron peel, coarsely chopped

50 g (2 oz) candied angelica, washed and diced

75 g (3 oz) glacé pineapple, washed and diced

grated rind of ½ lemon

175 g (6 oz) almonds, blanched and split

175 g (6 oz) butter

175 g (6 oz) caster sugar

3 eggs

225 g (8 oz) plain flour

Oven temperature: 150°C (300°F), Gas Mark 2

Prepare a 20 cm (8 inch) round cake tin by brushing with melted butter. Line with greaseproof paper.

Put the apricots into a large mixing bowl with the sultanas and the tea. Cover and leave overnight. Add all the fruit, nuts, and lemon rind to the bowl. Stir to mix.

Using a wooden spoon, an electric mixer or the double bladed knife in the food processor, beat the butter and sugar until very soft and creamy. Beat in one egg at a time. Stir in the flour.

Turn the whole of the cake mixture into the bowl of fruits. Stir to mix together thoroughly. Turn into the prepared tin and level the top with a palette knife. Tie a double thickness of brown paper around the outside of the tin.

Bake for 3 hours. Look at the cake after 1 hour and if the surface is beginning to brown lay a double thickness of brown paper over the top. Test with a skewer inserted into the centre of the cake after a total of 2½ hours. If it comes out clean the cake is baked.

Remove from the oven and leave to cool in the tin. Remove the outer wrapping, turn out of the tin, and peel off the lining paper. Wrap in greaseproof paper then in foil.

✳ This type of cake will keep well without freezing if stored in a cool dry place for not more than 6 weeks. Marzipan and ice the cake as directed on page 96.

LINING A DEEP CAKE TIN
Rich fruit cake mixtures need longer cooking than ordinary cakes; line the tin with a double thickness of greaseproof paper to prevent the sides burning.

Cut a strip of greaseproof paper long enough to fit all the way round the tin and wide enough to stand 5 cm (2 inch) above the rim of the tin when folded in half lengthways. Make a fold 1 cm (½ inch) along the long edge of the strip and snip at intervals of 2.5 cm (1 inch). Grease the tin and fit as shown.

Cut two circles of greaseproof paper to fit the base of the tin and place in position. Brush the lining paper with a little melted butter before pouring in the prepared cake mixture.

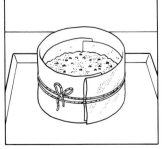

Wrap the tin in several thicknesses of brown paper and tie with string.

PLUG–IN·COOKING

From the toaster to the microwave cooker, small electric appliances not only save time and effort in the kitchen, they help you to prepare *consistently* good food. Today's designs are clean, neat and compact—in colours and styles that will complement the most traditional or modern kitchen.

The electric mixer takes all the hard work out of beating and whisking. Blenders complete otherwise laborious tasks, such as making mayonnaise and puréeing foods, at the flick of a switch. A more recent innovation, the food processor allows you to dice, shred, slice, grate and chop with ease, precision and phenomenal speed.

There are electric appliances for almost every culinary task. For deep-frying, the electric deep-fat fryer not only keeps the temperature of the oil constant to the setting you select, but its special filter lid retains odours and helps keep the kitchen clean.

For those who want to prepare quick hot snacks, the contact grill or electric sandwich maker can be used by even the most inexperienced cook. The contact grill keeps steaks and burgers moist and succulent, and the design of its ridged plates speeds the rate at which the food cooks. Toasted sandwich makers turn the humble sandwich into a meal, sealing in any number of tasty—sweet or savoury—fillings.

The slow cooker is the busy cook's best friend. The controlled gentle heat, means that dishes can be cooked during the day without any fear of spoiling and be ready to serve the moment you get home.

In contrast the microwave cooker, one of the newest kitchen appliances, is also the quickest. More and more cooks are discovering the microwave cooker's many assets: cooking entire meals, thawing and reheating straight from the freezer and cooking or reheating individual meals for latecomers. However, the microwave cooker can also help the busy cook with a whole host of other tasks, like softening butter or cream cheese for spreading, melting chocolate and gelatine, blanching vegetables before freezing and even toasting nuts. Once you begin to use the microwave, its value in the kitchen speaks for itself.

The recipes in this book quote timings for a 700 Watt output microwave cooker. If yours is a 500 Watt output cooker, add 20 seconds per minute to the calculated cooking time; for a 600 Watt output cooker, add 15 seconds per minute to the calculated cooking time.

Soufflé Omelette with Summer Fruits

SERVES 4

3 eggs, separated

½ tablespoon caster sugar

3 tablespoons cold water

15 g (½ oz) butter

cream, to serve (optional)

FILLING:
75 g (3 oz) raspberries, fresh or frozen
75 g (3 oz) caster sugar
40 g (1½ oz) blackcurrants, fresh or frozen

First make the filling. Put half the raspberries into a blender or food processor with 50 g (2 oz) of the sugar. Blend to a thick purée (the fruit does not need to be thawed if using frozen).

Have all the ingredients for the soufflé ready to make up just before serving. Stir together the egg yolks, sugar and water. Heat the butter in a deep frying pan, 15 cm (6 inch) in diameter, over moderate heat. Tilt the pan to coat all over with the butter. Warm a suitable serving plate and have the grill fully heated.

Whisk the egg whites stiffly with a food mixer or with a hand-held whisk. Quickly stir in the yolk mixture. Pour into the frying pan over moderate heat and cook for 10–12 minutes until the omelette puffs up to the top of the pan. Ease away from the edges with a palette knife all around. When the underside is lightly browned, transfer the pan to the grill. Cook for 2–3 minutes to brown lightly.

Mark across the centre of the omelette with a palette knife. Spoon half the filling over one half of the omelette and arrange the rest of the raspberries and all of the blackcurrants over it. Fold the other half of the omelette over. Slip the omelette on to the heated serving plate, or if easier, invert it. Sprinkle with the remaining sugar and serve immediately cut into quarters.

Serve the remaining filling separately as a sauce, topped with a little cream, if wished, and provide extra sugar.

Serving suggestion: For a spectacular end to an elegant meal, pour 2 tablespoons of brandy on to the plate around the omelette. Set alight and serve immediately.

Variation: Substitute fresh fruit in season for the raspberries and blackcurrants. Ripe peaches and apricots or juicy strawberries would make an excellent filling.

✳ Not suitable for freezing.

67

Left Soufflé omelette with summer fruits

Black and White Gâteau

SERVES 8–10

114 g (4 oz) butter
50 g (2 oz) cocoa
3 tablespoons milk
4 eggs
370 g (10 oz) caster sugar
1 teaspoon vanilla essence
170 g (6 oz) plain flour
½ teaspoon baking powder

FILLING AND DECORATION:
4 tablespoons caster sugar
2 teaspoons water
5 tablespoons rum
3 × 142 ml (5 fl oz) cartons whipping cream
142 g (5 oz) dark chocolate cake covering

Oven temperature: 160°C (325°F), Gas Mark 3
Grease three 20 cm (8 inch) sandwich tins and line the bases with greaseproof paper.

Put the butter, cocoa and milk into a small saucepan over low heat. Stir until melted and well mixed. Set aside.

Put the eggs, sugar and vanilla into a bowl and whisk, with a food mixer, until very light and creamy.

Whisk in the cocoa mixture. Sift the flour and baking powder over the surface and stir in well.

Divide the mixture equally among the tins. Bake for about 25 minutes or until lightly browned and springy to the touch. Cool on wire racks.

Put the sugar and water into a small saucepan over low heat. Stir to dissolve the sugar. Bring to the boil then turn the heat off and leave to bubble for a minute. Remove from the heat; stir in the rum. Pour one third of the rum syrup over each cake layer.

Whip the cream with a food mixer until soft peaks form. Sandwich the 3 cakes with whipped cream. Put the cake on a sheet of greaseproof paper. Spread more cream around the sides.

Finely grate about half the chocolate, and break the rest into a small bowl. Pat grated chocolate all over the sides of the cake with a palette knife. Add any remaining grated chocolate to the chocolate in the bowl. Place the bowl over a pan of simmering water. Stir until the chocolate has melted.

Spread the chocolate over the top of the cake. When set, decorate with the remaining cream.

* Freeze undecorated for up to 4 months or open freeze the decorated cake. Cover and freeze for up to 3 months. Thaw for 3–4 hours at room temperature.

Left Stilton dip, served with a selection of raw vegetables; **Right** Sardine sandwich spread, served with wholemeal bread

Stilton Dip

SERVES 4

100 g (4 oz) Stilton cheese, crumbled
225 g (8 oz) cream cheese or quark
2 tablespoons port
4 tablespoons milk
4 parsley sprigs, stalks removed

Place all the ingredients in a blender and blend until smooth. Or, press the Stilton and soft cheese through a sieve and mix in the port, milk and finely chopped parsley.

Spoon into a small bowl.

Serving suggestions: Serve with savoury biscuits, or a selection of crisp, raw vegetables cut into small pieces for dipping.

Variation: For a stronger flavour, use Danish Blue cheese instead of the Stilton.

✳ Freeze for up to 2 months. To serve, thaw overnight in the refrigerator or for 3–4 hours at room temperature.

≈ Microwave on DEFROST for 2–3 minutes to thaw. Allow to stand for 5 minutes.

Sardine Sandwich Spread

MAKES ENOUGH FOR 2 LARGE SANDWICHES

1 tablespoon snipped chives
1 spring onion, roughly chopped
large sprig of parsley
1 teaspoon grated horseradish
a little grated lemon rind
1 × 120 g (4½ oz) can sardines in oil, drained
1 teaspoon lemon juice, or to taste
2 tablespoons tomato purée
2 tablespoons soured cream
salt and black pepper

Put the chives, onion, parsley, horseradish and lemon rind in the blender. Cover, and blend for a few seconds. Scrape down then repeat.

Add the sardines, lemon juice, tomato purée and soured cream. Blend again, and scrape down. Add salt and pepper and blend for a few seconds until well mixed.

Note: Use immediately, or store in a covered container in the refrigerator. Use within 24 hours.

Variation: Substitute yogurt for the soured cream.

✳ Not suitable for freezing.

Tomato Hollandaise

MAKES 300 ml (½ pint)

175 g (6 oz) firm tomatoes, skinned, halved and seeded
3 egg yolks
100 g (4 oz) unsalted butter, melted
pinch of sugar
salt and black pepper

Dry the tomatoes inside and out with kitchen paper. Cut the flesh into small chunks and blend to a purée.

Mix the tomato purée and the egg yolks together in a bowl. Set the bowl over a saucepan of hot water. Cook, stirring frequently, over low heat until slightly thickened. Return to the blender.

Switch on the blender, gradually pour in the melted butter until it is all incorporated. Season to taste with sugar, salt and pepper. Serve warm.

Serving suggestions: Serve with poached white fish or poached eggs, or with a fish or cheese soufflé.

✳ Not suitable for freezing.

Above Blackberry fool, served with Palmier biscuits

Blackberry Fool

SERVES 4

350 g (12 oz) blackberries, hulled

50 g (2 oz) caster sugar

2 teaspoons lemon juice

1 × 284 ml (10 fl oz) carton double cream

Place the blackberries in a saucepan with the sugar and simmer gently for 5–8 minutes until softened. Remove from heat and leave to cool. Pour away any excess liquid. Place the blackberries in the blender and blend until smooth. Stir in the lemon juice.

Whip the cream until it forms soft peaks and fold in the blackberry purée. Spoon into a serving bowl and chill for 2–3 hours.

✳ Freeze for up to 1 month. Thaw for 4–5 hours in the refrigerator.

Blender Cream

MAKES 250 ml (9 fl oz)

150 g (5 oz) unsalted butter, cut in small pieces

120 ml (4 fl oz) milk

Put the butter in a small saucepan. Add the milk. Place over low heat, stirring frequently, until the butter is melted. Pour into the blender.

Blend for about 10 seconds then scrape down. Repeat 3 more times. Turn into a jar and cool. Cover and store in the refrigerator.

Note: Blender cream makes an excellent store-cupboard substitute for fresh double cream. Pour over fruit or puddings, or whip with an electric food mixer to piping consistency. Spread or pipe on to pastries and gâteaux.

✳ Not suitable for freezing.

Passion Cake

SERVES 10–12

150 g (5 oz) butter, cut into pieces

175 g (6 oz) soft brown sugar

2 eggs

200 g (7 oz) plain flour

2 teaspoons baking powder

1 teaspoon ground cinnamon

2 tablespoons milk

100 g (4 oz) stoned dates

50 g (2 oz) walnut halves or pieces

175 g (6 oz) carrots, trimmed and thinly peeled

ICING:
150 g (5 oz) cream cheese
150 g (5 oz) butter, softened
grated rind of 1 orange
200 g (7 oz) icing sugar

DECORATION:
6 walnut halves
6 dessert dates, stoned

Oven temperature: 180°C (350°F), Gas Mark 4

To make the cake, grease and base line two 19 cm (7½ inch) sandwich tins. Fit the double bladed knife into the processor. Process the butter and sugar for about 2 minutes until light and creamy. Scrape down once or twice during processing. Add the eggs one at a time, and process. Scrape down. Add the flour, baking powder, cinnamon, and milk. Process briefly to mix. Pour into a large mixing bowl.

Return the processor bowl and blade to the machine. Put the dates into the bowl. Process briefly to cut into pieces. Add the nuts and process again to the size required. Add the dates and nuts to the mixing bowl.

Replace the blade with the grating disc. Grate the carrots. Add the grated carrots to the cake mixture and stir all the ingredients together well. Divide equally between the prepared tins.

Bake for about 30 minutes or until springy to the touch. Cool on wire racks and peel off the lining paper.

To make the icing, put the cheese, butter and orange rind into the processor bowl and process until smooth. Gradually add the icing sugar to make a smooth soft consistency. Sandwich the two cakes with some of the icing. Use the rest to cover the top and sides. Decorate with walnuts and dates.

✳ Freeze the cakes before filling for up to 4 months. Thaw at room temperature in their wrappings for about 1 hour. Fill and decorate as above.

≈ Microwave on DEFROST for 5 minutes, turning over once. Allow to stand for 10 minutes. Fill and decorate as above.

French Onion Soup

SERVES 8

1.5 kg (3 lb) onions

100 ml (3 fl oz) vegetable oil

1.75 litres (3 pints) stock

salt and black pepper

3–4 tablespoons sherry

TOPPING:
225 g (8 oz) Gruyère cheese
1 teaspoon French mustard
2 cloves garlic, crushed
2 tablespoons vegetable oil
8 thick slices of French bread

Fit the slicing disc to the processor and put the lid in position. If necessary, cut the onions in half so they will fit into the feed tube. Pack as many as possible into the tube at a time and force down with the pusher while the machine is operating. Continue until the onions are all sliced.

Heat the oil in a large, deep frying pan over low heat. Add the onions and stir to coat with the oil. Cook uncovered for about 45 minutes, stirring frequently, until the onions are a rich dark brown. Add the stock; cover, and simmer for 30 minutes. Add salt and pepper and sherry to taste.

Fit the grating disc to the processor and put the lid in position. Cut the block of cheese to fit the tube. Force down with the pusher to grate the cheese while the machine operates. Remove the lid and the disc. Add the mustard and garlic to the cheese, and stir the oil in with a fork.

Spread the cheese mixture on to the bread. Put a layer of onions in 8 ovenproof bowls. Set a piece of bread on top of each. Spoon the soup over. When the bread rises to the surface, place the bowls under a preheated medium grill. Grill for 5–7 minutes until bubbling and browned. Serve immediately.

Note: The soup may be stored in a closely covered container in the refrigerator for 2–3 days.

✳ Freeze for up to 1 month in small containers for quicker thawing. To serve, reheat gently from frozen. When thawed bring to the boil. Lower the heat and simmer for at least 3 minutes.

≈ Microwave on HIGH for 8–10 minutes, breaking down the block as it thaws. Allow to stand for 5 minutes. Reheat on HIGH for 10 minutes, stirring once.

Slaw with Mayonnaise

SERVES 4

175 g (6 oz) firm white cabbage

50 g (2 oz) onion

100 g (4 oz) carrots

MAYONNAISE:
1 egg yolk
1 tablespoon wine vinegar
salt and black pepper
150 ml (¼ pint) olive oil

1 tablespoon chopped parsley, to garnish

First make the mayonnaise. Fit the double bladed knife into the processor bowl. Add the egg yolk, vinegar, and salt and pepper. Put the lid in position and add the oil in a very slow continuous stream through the feed tube while the machine is operating. Stop the machine and scrape down the bowl once or twice. The whole process should take 2½–3 minutes. Adjust the seasoning to taste.

Remove about half the mayonnaise and store in a screw-topped jar in the refrigerator, for another occasion. Remove the double blade, and replace it with the slicing disc. Put the lid back into position.

Cut the cabbage into wedges to fit into the feed tube. Force down with the pusher while the machine is operating. Process the onion in the same way.

Replace the slicing disc with the grating disc. Put the lid in position and pack with carrots in the upright position. Force down with the pusher while the machine is operating.

All the vegetables will be sliced or shredded into the mayonnaise in 2–3 minutes. Remove the lid and stir the ingredients together then season to taste. If liked, more mayonnaise may be stirred in. Turn into a salad bowl. Chill for 30 minutes, then sprinkle with chopped parsley before serving.

Note: The quantities for the vegetables are only approximate and can be varied according to taste.

Serving suggestion: For a quick summer lunch serve with a selection of cold meats and crunchy radishes. Hot garlic bread goes well with this lunch.

✳ Not suitable for freezing.

Below Slaw with mayonnaise, served with radishes and a selection of cold meats

Tabbouleh

SERVES 4

100 g (4 oz) cracked wheat (bulgar, pourgouri or burghul)

150 ml (¼ pint) cold water

2 large spring onions, cut in large pieces

15 g (½ oz) large leaved parsley

15 g (½ oz) fresh mint

2 tablespoons olive oil

3 tablespoons lemon juice

salt and black pepper

100 g (4 oz) cherry tomatoes, quartered

TO GARNISH:
mint sprigs
a lemon wedge

Put the cracked wheat into a bowl with the water. Leave to soak for 30 minutes until the wheat absorbs all the water and swells to about twice its bulk.

Place the spring onions, parsley, mint, olive oil and lemon juice into the food processor bowl. Process for a few seconds to chop the onions and herbs, then mix with the cracked wheat. Season to taste with salt and pepper and stir in the tomatoes. Garnish with mint sprigs and a lemon wedge.

Serving suggestions: Serve with thick slices of sesame seed bread and butter if liked. Serve with kebabs or as a snack with Greek Feta cheese.

Variation: Use a few chopped fresh coriander leaves, when available, instead of the mint.

✳ Not suitable for freezing.

Left Tabbouleh, garnished with mint and lemon

Spaghetti Courgettes with Garlic

SERVES 4

450 g (1 lb) courgettes

2 tablespoons chopped fresh dill or 1 teaspoon dried dill

4–5 cloves garlic

50 g (2 oz) butter

salt and black pepper

Trim the courgettes. Fit the coarse shredding disc to the processor and put the lid in position. Pack the tube firmly with courgettes, standing upright to give shorter shreds. Force down with the pusher while the machine is operating. Repeat until all have been shredded. Remove to a bowl.

Replace the disc with the double bladed knife. Put the dill and the garlic into the bowl and process until finely chopped. Stir into the courgettes.

Heat the butter in a large frying pan over medium heat. When it begins to brown, stir in the vegetables. Fry, stirring, for about 2 minutes, or until well heated through. Season to taste and serve immediately.

Serving suggestions: Serve with meat, fish or poultry or with a vegetable quiche as part of a non-meat meal.

✳ Not suitable for freezing.

Swiss Steak

SERVES 4

2 tablespoons vegetable oil

2 large cloves garlic, crushed

2 medium onions, sliced

750 g (1½ lb) chuck steak in 1 or 2 pieces

4 tablespoons flour

salt and black pepper

2 tablespoons paprika

2 × 397 g (14 oz) cans tomatoes

Below: Top Apple drop scones; **Bottom** Quick and easy doughnuts

Put the oil into the multicooker and turn the heat to setting 1. Add the garlic to the pan with the onions. Cover the pan but leave the vent open. Cook for about 10 minutes to soften the vegetables and extract the flavour.

Trim the meat and pat dry with kitchen paper but leave in 1 or 2 large pieces. Lay on top of the onions. Sprinkle with the flour, salt and pepper and the paprika. Pour the tomatoes and their juices on top.

Cover the pan and close the vent. Cook on the setting between 'simmer' and 1 to keep gently bubbling for about 1 hour. Turn the meat and if necessary, add a little water to prevent sticking. Cook covered for a further 30–45 minutes or until tender.

Transfer the meat to a hot serving dish. Cut into 4 steaks. Spoon the sauce and vegetables over and serve immediately.

✳ Freeze for up to 1 month. Place in an ovenproof dish, cover and cook in a 150°C (325°F), Gas Mark 3 oven for about 45 minutes.

≈ Microwave on DEFROST for 20 minutes to thaw. Allow to stand for 5 minutes. Microwave on HIGH for 6–8 minutes to reheat.

Apple Drop Scones

MAKES 12

vegetable oil, for brushing

100 g (4 oz) self-raising flour

½ teaspoon ground cinnamon

2 tablespoons caster sugar

25 g (1 oz) butter

75 g (3 oz) cooking apple, pared, cored and finely chopped

1 egg

about 120 ml (4 fl oz) milk

Brush the bottom of the multicooker with a little oil. Cover, close the vent, and heat on setting 4.

Sift the dry ingredients into a large bowl. Rub the butter in with the fingertips until the mixture resembles fine crumbs. Stir in the apple. Make a well in the centre. Break the egg in and gradually stir in the milk to make a batter.

Open the cooker. Drop spoonfuls of the batter into the pan, cooking 5–6 at a time. For oval scones, drop from the side of the spoon, for round scones drop from the tip. Cook, uncovered, for about 1½ minutes until browned on the underside and the bubbles on the surface begin to break. Turn and cook the other side until browned.

Transfer to a wire rack covered with a clean tea towel. Fold the towel over to cover while the rest of the scones are cooked. Serve warm or cold.

✳ Not suitable for freezing.

French-fried Eggs

SERVES 6

6 eggs

COATING SAUCE:
50 g (2 oz) butter
75 g (3 oz) mushrooms, finely chopped
3 tablespoons flour
1 × 284 ml (10 fl oz) carton single cream
salt and black pepper
ground mace

CRUMB COATING:
flour, to dust
1 egg
100 g (4 oz) fine dry breadcrumbs
oil, for deep frying

COURGETTE PURÉE:
350 g (12 oz) courgettes, sliced
2 tablespoons finely chopped fresh dill
¼ teaspoon salt
3 tablespoons double cream

Place the eggs in a deep pan of boiling water. Bring back to the boil. Cook for 5 minutes. Drain, then run cold water over for 3–4 minutes to cool. Carefully remove the shells and put the eggs back into a pan of cold water.

To make the sauce, melt the butter in a medium saucepan over low heat. Add the mushrooms. Stir and cook for about 3 minutes to soften. Sprinkle the flour over the mushrooms and stir in. Gradually stir in the cream. Cook, stirring, for about 3 minutes until very thick. Season to taste with salt, pepper and a little mace.

Drain the eggs then gently scoop the sauce up around each egg to coat completely. Chill for 30–45 minutes.

Dust the coated eggs lightly with flour. Whisk the raw egg and a little water together with a fork in a small bowl. Put some of the crumbs into a second small dish. Working with one egg at a time: roll in the beaten egg, drain, roll in the crumbs. Pat and roll gently in the hands then repeat the egging and crumbing for a second time. Set into the frying basket. Treat the rest of the eggs in the same way, using extra crumbs as necessary.

Pour the oil into the deep fryer. Cover, and turn the setting to 190°C (375°F).

While the oil is heating, prepare the courgette purée. Put the courgettes, dill and salt into a medium saucepan with a little water to just cover the bottom of the pan. Put the pan over medium heat, cover and cook for 3–4 minutes or until tender. Drain the courgettes and put into a blender or food processor with the cream and blend to a purée. Return to the pan, place over low heat and keep hot until ready to serve.

Remove the lid from the fryer. Lower the basket with the eggs into the oil. Cover the pan and cook for 1½ minutes. Remove the lid and lift the basket out.

With a slotted spoon place each egg on to crumpled kitchen paper. Serve immediately set on a bed of the courgette purée.

Serving suggestion: Serve as a first course.

✳ Not suitable for freezing.

Quick and Easy Doughnuts

MAKES 13–14 RINGS

225 g (8 oz) self-raising flour

¼ teaspoon grated nutmeg

50 g (2 oz) caster sugar

25 g (1 oz) butter

1 egg

about 4 tablespoons milk

oil, for deep frying

caster sugar, for coating

Sift the flour, nutmeg and sugar into a mixing bowl. Rub in the butter with the fingertips until the mixture resembles fine crumbs. Whisk the egg and milk together; stir quickly into the dry ingredients to make a soft dough. Turn out on to a board lightly dusted with self-raising flour.

Pour the oil into the fryer. Cover, and set the control to 160°C (325°F).

Lightly knead the dough to a smooth soft mixture which rolls easily. Roll out the dough to about 1 cm (½ inch) thick. Cut into 6 cm (2½ inch) rounds with a sharp scone cutter. Cut out the centres with a 2.5 cm (1 inch) cutter.

Carefully lay about half the doughnuts in the frying basket. Remove the lid and lower the basket into the oil. Cover the pan and cook for 1½ minutes. Turn the doughnuts. Cover and cook the other side for 1–1½ minutes.

Remove the doughnuts immediately and drain on crumpled kitchen paper. Roll in sugar. Cook the rest in the same way.

Serving suggestion: Serve while still warm or on the same day.

✳ Not suitable for freezing.

COATING FRENCH-FRIED EGGS

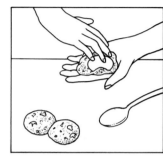

Work a portion of the mushroom mixture around each egg, so that it is completely enclosed.

Dust the coated eggs with flour; dip in beaten egg and roll in breadcrumbs. Repeat for a thicker coating.

75

Country Beef Casserole

SERVES 4–6

2 medium carrots, sliced
2 medium onions, sliced
1 medium parsnip, sliced
6 black peppercorns
1 large bay leaf
½ teaspoon salt
sprig of fresh thyme
1.25 kg (2½ lb) shin beef, cut into thick slices
300 ml (½ pint) dry cider

Put the vegetables into the cooking pot and stir in the peppercorns, bay leaf, salt and thyme. Lay the slices of meat on top and pour the cider over. Cover and leave in a cool place overnight.

Drain off the marinade into a saucepan and bring to the boil. Pour over the meat, cover, and cook on HIGH heat for 5–6 hours.

✳ Freeze for up to 3 months. Thaw at room temperature for 2 hours. Reheat gently on the hob for about 45 minutes.

≈ Microwave on DEFROST for 20 minutes to thaw. Microwave on HIGH for 10–12 minutes to reheat, stirring once.

Sauerbraten

SERVES 6–8

1.75 kg (4–4½ lb) topside
150 ml (¼ pint) red wine
2 cloves garlic, sliced
150 ml (¼ pint) red wine vinegar
2 carrots, sliced
1 medium onion, sliced
6 cloves
2 tablespoons soft dark brown sugar
1 tablespoon juniper berries, crushed
2 bay leaves
1 teaspoon mustard powder
½ tablespoon cornflour, blended with a little water
2 tablespoons seedless raisins
salt and black pepper

Put the beef into a glass or earthenware bowl into which it just fits. Put the wine, wine vinegar, carrots, garlic and onion in a saucepan. Add the cloves, sugar, juniper berries, bay leaves and mustard powder and bring slowly to the boil, stirring all the time. Pour over the beef and leave to cool, then cover and marinate in the refrigerator for 3–4 days. Turn the beef in the marinade once or twice a day.

When ready to cook, remove the meat from the marinade and pat dry with kitchen paper. Strain the marinade into a measuring jug and make up to 300 ml (½ pint) with water if necessary. Fry the beef in its own fat over moderate heat in a large heavy frying pan until browned on all sides, then place in the slow cooker.

Pour the marinade into a saucepan and bring to the boil. Pour over the meat; cover and cook on HIGH for 6 hours without lifting the lid.

Transfer the beef to a warmed serving platter and leave to stand in a warm place for about 15 minutes (this makes the meat easier to slice).

Skim or blot off surplus fat from the cooking liquid. Pour into a saucepan and boil rapidly to reduce slightly. Stir the cornflour into the liquid with the raisins, add salt and pepper to taste. Simmer until thickened, stirring constantly. Serve the beef sliced, with the sauce poured over.

✳ The beef can be frozen in the marinade for up to 3 months, but it is so bulky that it may not be worth the freezer space. It should be marinated for a further 2 days after defrosting in the refrigerator.

Steamed Pear and Syrup Pudding

SERVES 4–6

3 tablespoons golden syrup

411 g (14½ oz) can pear halves, drained

100 g (4 oz) sugar

175 g (6 oz) self-raising flour

¾ teaspoon mixed spice

100 g (4 oz) butter or margarine

about 2 tablespoons milk

2 eggs

Put the cooking pot into the cooker and set the lid in place. Turn the setting to HIGH to heat while the pudding is made.

Put the syrup in a 900 ml (1½ pint) buttered pudding bowl. Arrange the pear halves over the bottom and half-way up the sides of the bowl. Mix the sugar, flour, and spice together. Rub in the butter or margarine. Whisk together the milk and eggs and stir in to make a smooth soft dropping consistency.

Spoon the mixture into the prepared bowl. Cover closely with foil and set the bowl into the cooker. Pour boiling water into the pot to come about half way up the sides of the bowl. Cover the cooker and leave to cook for 5–8 hours.

Turn the pudding out and serve.

✳ Freeze for up to 3 months. To serve, thaw at room temperature for 4 hours. Reheat by steaming for 1–1½ hours

Left Sauerbraten in marinade

77

Bread and Butter Pudding

SERVES 6

50 g (2 oz) butter

10 thin large slices brown bread, crusts removed

grated rind of 1 large orange

50 g (2 oz) preserved ginger, finely chopped

500 ml (18 fl oz) milk

500 ml (18 fl oz) single cream

5 eggs

50 g (2 oz) caster sugar

5 tablespoons Cointreau

Butter the inside of the cooking pot. Spread the slices of bread with butter. Cut each slice in four. Arrange a layer buttered side down in the pot and the rest of the bread in layers buttered side up, sprinkling each layer with the orange rind and chopped ginger.

Whisk the remaining ingredients. Strain over the bread. Set the pot into the cooker; put the lid in place. Switch to HIGH; leave for 4–5 hours until cooked.

Remove the lid and brown the pudding under a preheated hot grill for 2–3 minutes.

✳ Not suitable for freezing.

Apples in Wine

SERVES 6

6 medium cooking apples, peeled and cored

about 75 g (3 oz) caster sugar

cinnamon stick broken into 6 pieces

275 ml (9 fl oz) sweet white wine

Butter the bottom of the cooking pot. Set the apples in place and fill the centres with sugar. Insert a piece of cinnamon in each. Pour the wine over.

Set the pot into the cooker and put the lid in place. Switch to HIGH and cook for 3½–4½ hours until tender. Discard the cinammon and serve.

Serving suggestion: Serve the apples hot or cold with their juices and single cream to pour over them.

✳ Freeze for up to 3 months. To serve, thaw at room temperature for 4 hours.

Nutty Burgers

SERVES 2

275 g (10 oz) lean minced beef

2 tablespoons natural yogurt

50 g (2 oz) onion, finely chopped

2 tablespoons finely chopped parsley

2 cloves garlic, finely chopped

1 teaspoon coriander seeds, crushed

salt and black pepper

25 g (1 oz) salted peanuts, coarsely chopped

oil, for brushing

Put the meat into a mixing bowl with all the other ingredients except the nuts and oil. Season generously with salt and pepper. Knead to mix thoroughly.

Heat the contact grill.

Divide the mixture into 8 equal parts. Shape into balls and press flat into rounds about 6 cm (2½ inch) in diameter. Press the peanuts over 4 of the rounds. Stack a second round on top of each. Press together.

Brush the top of each burger sandwich with oil. Invert on to the grill. Brush the second side with oil. Close the lid, but do not press too firmly. Cook for 5–6 minutes.

Transfer to heated plates and serve immediately.

Serving suggestion: Serve with grilled oven chips and a green salad dressed with natural yogurt and snipped chives. A selection of relishes such as cucumber or sweetcorn go well with these burgers.

✳ Freeze the uncooked burgers for up to 2 months. To serve, thaw at room temperature for 2–3 hours then cook as above.

Griddle Scones

MAKES 8

225 g (8 oz) self-raising flour

¼ teaspoon salt

25 g (1 oz) white fat

¼ teaspoon bicarbonate of soda

1 × 150 g (5.29 oz) carton natural yogurt

about 2 teaspoons milk

Mix the flour and salt together in a mixing bowl. Rub the fat in with the fingertips until the mixture resembles fine crumbs. Mix the bicarbonate into the yogurt until it froths well. Stir into the flour immediately, adding a little milk if necessary to form a dough which comes away cleanly from the bowl.

Heat the contact grill.

Turn the dough on to a lightly floured surface and knead gently until smooth. Roll to a rectangle 20 × 10 cm (8 × 4 inches). Cut with a sharp knife into 8 equal squares.

Open the grill and place as many scones on to the base as it will take without crowding. Cook with the lid open for about 6 minutes until the undersides are well browned. Turn the scones. Cook the second side for 6 minutes to brown. Transfer to a wire rack to cool slightly.

Serving suggestion: Serve while still warm, with butter and honey, jam, marmalade, or soft cheese.

✳ Freeze the cooked scones for up to 6 months. To serve, thaw at room temperature for 1 hour then cook in a 180°C (350°F), Gas Mark 4 oven for 5–10 minutes until warm.

Prune Pies

MAKES 4

1 × 368 g (13 oz) packet frozen shortcrust pastry, thawed

FILLING:
225 g (8 oz) pitted prunes, chopped
grated rind of 1 large orange
6 tablespoons orange juice
6 tablespoons water
50 g (2 oz) soft brown sugar
½ teaspoon grated nutmeg

To make the filling, put the prunes in a medium saucepan with the other ingredients. Simmer over low heat, stirring frequently, for about 10 minutes to make a thick paste. Set aside to cool.

Heat the contact grill.

Cut the pastry into 4 equal pieces. Roll each on a lightly floured board to a rectangle 23 × 10 cm (9 × 4 inches). Spread a quarter of the filling over one half of each pastry strip, leaving a margin of 1 cm (½ inch). Brush the edges with water then fold the pastry over the filling. Press the edges to seal.

Carefully set the pies into place on the base of the grill: 2 or 4 at a time depending on the grill size. Cook with the lid open for about 6 minutes to brown underneath. Turn the pastries carefully. Cook for a further 6 minutes to brown the second side.

Transfer to a wire rack to cool.

Serving suggestion: Serve warm or cold, with cream, ice cream, or custard.

✳ Open freeze until firm, then pack in a rigid container. Freeze for up to 6 months. To serve, thaw at room temperature for 2–3 hours.

≈ Microwave on DEFROST for 10 minutes, rearranging twice. Allow to stand for 5–10 minutes.

Left Stuffed pork fillet, garnished with mange-tout peas and sliced mushrooms

Stuffed Pork Fillet

SERVES 2

350 g (12 oz) pork fillet

25 g (1 oz) butter, melted

STUFFING:
75 g (3 oz) button mushrooms
1 teaspoon mustard
1 tablespoon finely chopped parsley
2 tablespoons grated Parmesan cheese
1 clove garlic, finely chopped
salt and black pepper

TO GARNISH:
mange-tout peas, cooked
sliced mushrooms, cooked

Cut the fillet across into 8 equal slices. Brush the meat on either side with butter.

Finely chop the mushrooms. Mix with the mustard, parsley, cheese, garlic and salt and pepper to taste.

Heat the contact grill. Stack the slices of meat in pairs. Place on the base of the grill. Close the lid and cook for 1 minute to brown lightly. Separate the pairs of slices, turning the browned side up.

Divide the filling equally among half the slices and cover with the remaining slices. Close the lid and cook for 4 minutes.

Garnish the meat with the mange-tout peas and mushrooms and serve immediately.

Serving suggestions: Serve with baked jacket potatoes or tiny new potatoes in their skins.

✳ Not suitable for freezing.

Breakfast Sandwiches

SERVES 2

4 large slices bread
25 g (1 oz) butter
2 eggs
salt and black pepper
2 slices ham, about 75 g (3 oz)
2 slices cheese, about 50 g (2 oz)

Heat the sandwich toaster. Spread one side of each slice of bread with the butter. Press 2 slices buttered side down on to the base of the toaster. Press down in the centre with a large spoon to make an indentation.

Break an egg into each hollow. Season lightly with salt and pepper. Lay a slice of ham over the top of each egg, then a slice of cheese. Cover with the remaining bread, buttered side up.

Close the lid and cook for about 3 minutes until well browned. Remove and serve immediately.

Serving suggestion: These sandwiches make a delicious hot breakfast or brunch snack. Serve with freshly squeezed orange juice or a selection of fresh fruit for a quick, nutritious start to the day.

✷ Not suitable for freezing.

Chop Suey Triangles

SERVES 2

25 g (1 oz) beansprouts
1 large spring onion, sliced
1 tablespoon snipped chives
25 g (1 oz) cucumber, diced
4 mange-tout peas, topped, tailed and sliced across
1 small piece root ginger, peeled and chopped
1 egg, beaten
salt and black pepper
4 large slices bread
25 g (1 oz) butter

Mix all the vegetables and the ginger. Pour the egg over the vegetables and add salt and pepper.

Heat the sandwich toaster. Spread one side of each slice of bread with the butter. Press 2 slices of bread, buttered side down, on to the base of the toaster. Pile the filling in the centres and spread out to within 1 cm (½ inch) of the edge. Cover with the remaining bread buttered side up.

Close the lid and cook for 2–3 minutes until browned. Remove and serve immediately.

✷ Not suitable for freezing.

German Hot Dogs

SERVES 2

4 large slices bread
25 g (1 oz) butter
50 g (2 oz) Emmenthal cheese, sliced
75 g (3 oz) sauerkraut, drained
black pepper
1 × 225 g (8 oz) can hot dog sausages, drained
German mustard

Heat the sandwich toaster. Spread one side of each slice of bread with the butter. Press 2 slices, buttered side down, on to the base of the sandwich toaster. Lay half the cheese on each. Cover in the centre with sauerkraut and season lightly with pepper.

Cut the sausages in half lengthways. Lay on top of the sauerkraut. Spread with mustard to taste. Cover with the remaining bread, buttered side up. Close the lid and cook for 2–3 minutes until browned. Serve immediately.

✷ Not suitable for freezing.

Mushroom Butties

SERVES 2

50 g (2 oz) butter
1 large clove garlic, crushed
1 tablespoon finely chopped parsley
1 tablespoon finely chopped thyme or chives
4 large slices bread
2 very large field or flat mushrooms
salt and black pepper

Put half the butter into a small saucepan over low heat. Add the garlic and the herbs. Heat very gently. Heat the sandwich toaster. Spread the remaining butter on one side of each slice of bread. Place two slices, buttered side down on to the sandwich toaster.

Place a mushroom on each of 2 slices, season to taste with salt and pepper and pour a little of the melted butter over each. Cover with the remaining slices of bread, buttered side up, close the lid and cook for 2–3 minutes to brown. Remove and serve immediately.

✷ Not suitable for freezing.

Italian Cheese Toasties

SERVES 2

4 large slices bread

25 g (1 oz) butter

½ teaspoon garlic purée

25 g (1 oz) salami, thinly sliced

75 g (3 oz) Mozzarella cheese, sliced

50 g (2 oz) tomatoes, sliced

4 black olives, stoned and sliced

pinch of oregano

salt and black pepper

Heat the sandwich toaster. Spread one side of each slice of bread with the butter. Spread the unbuttered side of 2 slices with the garlic purée; press buttered side down on to the base of the toaster.

Cover each with a layer of salami, then cheese, and finally tomato. Sprinkle the olives over the top and add a little oregano and salt and pepper. Cover with the remaining bread buttered side up.

Close the lid and cook for 2–3 minutes until browned. Remove and serve immediately.

✳ Not suitable for freezing.

Above Italian cheese toasties

81

Chocolate Nut Pockets

SERVES 4

50 g (2 oz) almonds, finely chopped

25 g (1 oz) honey

75 g (3 oz) dark chocolate, broken into bits

4 large slices white bread

25 g (1 oz) butter

2 tablespoons caster sugar

Put the nuts, honey and chocolate into a small bowl. Set over a pan of hot, not boiling, water. Stir until the chocolate and honey are just melted and the ingredients well mixed. Remove from the heat.

Heat the sandwich toaster. Butter one side of each slice of bread. Sprinkle with sugar. Press 2 slices buttered side down on to the base of the toaster.

Pile the filling in the centres and spread to within 1 cm (½ inch) of the edge. Cover with the remaining bread,buttered side up.

Close the lid and cook for 2–3 minutes until browned. Remove and serve immediately.

✳ Not suitable for freezing.

Tropical Toasts

SERVES 4

4 large slices wholewheat bread

25 g (1 oz) butter

1 banana, 125 g (5 oz) weight before peeling

½ teaspoon lemon juice

50 g (2 oz) stoned dates, finely chopped

50 g (2 oz) cottage cheese

25 g (1 oz) caster sugar

½ teaspoon ground cinnamon

Spread one side of each slice of bread with the butter. Heat the sandwich toaster. Peel and mash the banana. Stir in the lemon juice, dates and cheese.

Press 2 slices of the bread, buttered side down, on to the base of the toaster. Pile the filling in the centres. Cover with remaining bread, buttered side up.

Close the lid and cook for 2–3 minutes until browned. Remove and sprinkle with a mixture of sugar and cinnamon. Serve immediately.

✳ Not suitable for freezing.

Right Cock-a-leekie soup, served with oatcakes

Cock-a-leekie Soup

SERVES

3 chicken quarters

salt and black pepper

1 bay leaf

1 bouquet garni

4 leeks, trimmed and sliced

25 g (1 oz) long-grain rice

750 ml (1¼ pints) chicken stock

1 tablespoon chopped parsley, to garnish

Arrange the chicken pieces in a circle in a shallow dish. Cover with clingfilm and pierce. Cook on HIGH for 12–14 minutes, turning the pieces over halfway through cooking. Allow to stand.

Meanwhile, place the remaining ingredients with 300 ml (½ pint) of the stock in a large bowl and cook on HIGH for 10 minutes, stirring once during cooking.

Skin the cooked chicken, reserving all the cooking juices. Cut the meat from the bones and add to the tureen with the remaining stock and cooking juices. Cook on HIGH for 10 minutes. Remove the bouquet garni and sprinkle with chopped parsley.

Variation: Add 50 g (2 oz) soaked prunes to the soup.

✱ Pack in a rigid container allowing a 1 cm (½ inch) headspace. Freeze for up to 1 month.

≈ Microwave on HIGH for 8–10 minutes, breaking down the block as it thaws. Allow to stand for 10 minutes. Microwave on HIGH for 4–6 minutes to reheat.

Creamed Mushroom Ramekins

SERVES 4

100 g (4 oz) button mushrooms, quartered

1 small clove garlic, crushed

3 spring onions, chopped

15 g (½ oz) butter

salt and black pepper

1 × 142 ml (5 fl oz) carton double cream

3 eggs, beaten

75 g (3 oz) mature Cheddar cheese, grated

½ teaspoon paprika

1 tablespoon grated Parmesan cheese

sprigs of parsley, to garnish

Place mushrooms, garlic, onions and butter in a shallow glass dish. Cook on HIGH for 3 minutes. Add salt and pepper. Divide the mushroom mixture equally between 4 small ramekin dishes.

Beat together the cream, eggs, Cheddar cheese and paprika. Pour over the mushrooms. Place the ramekins in the microwave cooker, spaced out evenly. Cook on HIGH for 5 minutes. Sprinkle with Parmesan cheese. Place under a preheated grill for a few minutes to colour or sprinkle with a little more paprika. Garnish with sprigs of fresh parsley.

Variation: Replace mushrooms with cooked prawns.

✱ Not suitable for freezing.

Chicken Liver Pâté

SERVES 4

225 g (8 oz) chicken livers, trimmed and sliced

225 g (8 oz) streaky bacon, rinded and chopped

50 g (2 oz) button mushrooms, chopped

1 clove garlic, chopped

1 onion, chopped

100 g (4 oz) butter

1 teaspoon dried mixed herbs

salt and black pepper

pinch of ground mace

2 tablespoons brandy

TO GARNISH:
50 g (2 oz) butter, melted
bay leaves
black peppercorns

Place the chicken livers, bacon, mushrooms, garlic and onion in a large bowl. Cover and cook on HIGH for 10 minutes, stirring twice. Drain off all but 1 tablespoon juices.

Place the butter in a small bowl with the herbs, salt, pepper and mace. Cook on HIGH for 45 seconds.

Sieve the liver mixture and butter mixture with the brandy or place in a blender or food processor and blend until smooth. Pour into a greased 600 ml (1 pint) straight-sided round dish. Cook on HIGH for 8 minutes. Cool, then chill.

To garnish, pour melted butter over the surface, add bay leaves and peppercorns and allow to set.

✱ Freeze for up to 3 weeks. Thaw overnight in the refrigerator.

≈ Microwave on DEFROST for 6 minutes. Leave to stand for 1 hour before serving.

Hot Herb Bread

SERVES 4–6

50 g (2 oz) butter

1 tablespoon chopped mixed fresh herbs, or
2 teaspoons dried mixed herbs

25 cm (10 inch) piece cut from a French stick

Place the butter in a bowl and add the herbs. Cook on DEFROST until softened – about 30 seconds.

Make diagonal cuts at 2 cm (1 inch) intervals almost through to the base of the loaf and spread each side of these slices with the herb butter. Spread any leftover butter along the top and sides of the loaf.

Wrap the loaf in greaseproof paper or clingfilm and cook on HIGH for 1 minute 10 seconds. Unwrap and serve as an accompaniment to soups or salads.

✱ Not suitable for freezing.

Garlic Croûtons

SERVES 4

25 g (1 oz) butter

1 clove garlic, crushed

½ teaspoon ground coriander (optional)

1 thick slice of bread from a large white or brown loaf

Place the butter, garlic and coriander, if used, in a bowl and cook on HIGH for 40 seconds, until melted. Trim the crusts from the bread and cut the slices into neat 1 cm (½ inch) cubes. Toss in the melted butter and cook on HIGH for 1 minute. Stir and cook on HIGH for a further minute. Stand for 2 minutes.

✱ Not suitable for freezing.

Sherried Kidneys

SERVES 4

8 lambs' kidneys, about 350 g (12 oz), cored, skinned and halved

black pepper

1 teaspoon Worcestershire sauce

4 rashers streaky bacon, rinded and chopped

1 clove garlic, crushed

1 onion, chopped

25 g (1 oz) butter

1 tablespoon flour

300 ml (½ pint) beef stock

2 tablespoons chopped fresh parsley

2 tablespoons dry sherry

1 bay leaf

TO GARNISH:
sprigs of parsley
triangles of fried bread

Below Scampi Provençale, served on a bed of boiled rice

Place the kidneys in a shallow dish. Add the pepper and Worcestershire sauce. Cover and cook on HIGH for 4 minutes; add the bacon and cook on HIGH for a further 5 minutes, stirring once. Keep hot.

Mix the garlic, onion and butter in a bowl. Cook on HIGH for 1 minute. Stir in the flour and cook on HIGH for 1 minute. Whisk in the stock, parsley and sherry. Add the bay leaf. Cook on HIGH for 3 minutes, whisking once during cooking.

Pour the sauce over the kidneys and bacon. Cover and cook on HIGH for 2 minutes. Remove bay leaf. Serve garnished with parsley and fried bread.

Serving suggestion: Serve with creamed potatoes and glazed small onions.

✳ Freeze for up to 2 months.

≋ Microwave on DEFROST for 6–8 minutes. Allow to stand for 10 minutes. Cover and cook on HIGH for 4–5 minutes to reheat, stirring once.

Scampi Provençale

SERVES 4

1 onion, finely chopped

1 clove garlic, crushed

25 g (1 oz) butter

1 × 397 g (14 oz) can chopped tomatoes

2 tablespoons dry white wine

½ teaspoon dried oregano

1 tablespoon tomato purée

1 teaspoon sugar

few drops Tabasco sauce

1 tablespoon cornflour, blended with 2 teaspoons water

salt and black pepper

450 g (1 lb) peeled scampi, thawed if frozen

sprigs of fresh parsley, to garnish

Place the onion, garlic and butter in a large shallow, casserole dish. Cover and cook on HIGH for 2 minutes. Stir in the chopped tomatoes, wine, oregano, tomato purée, sugar, Tabasco sauce, blended cornflour, salt and pepper. Cook on HIGH for 5 minutes. Stir in the scampi. Cook for a further 4 minutes. Garnish with parsley and serve.

Serving suggestion: Serve with a green salad.

Variation: Substitute prawns for the scampi.

✳ Freeze for up to 1 month.

≋ Microwave on DEFROST for 10 minutes, breaking down the block as it thaws. Allow to stand for 5 minutes. Mirowave on HIGH for 2–3 minutes to reheat, stirring once.

Dijon Liver

SERVES 4

1 tablespoon oil
2 small onions, cut into rings
25 g (1 oz) butter
350 g (12 oz) lamb's liver, cut into thin strips
150 ml (¼ pint) beef stock
2 teaspoons cornflour, blended with 2 tablespoons of water
1 teaspoon chopped parsley
1 tablespoon French mustard
grated rind and juice of 1 orange
salt and black pepper

Pour the oil into a heatproof bowl. Heat on HIGH for 1 minute. Add the onions, cover with clingfilm and puncture. Microwave on HIGH for 3 minutes. Arrange the onions in a large shallow dish.

Place the butter in the bowl and microwave on HIGH for 1 minute. Stir the liver into the hot butter. Cover with clingfilm and puncture. Microwave on HIGH for 3 minutes. Add to the onions.

Place the stock, cornflour, parsley, French mustard, orange rind and juice and salt and pepper to taste in a 1 litre (1¾ pint) jug. Stir well. Microwave on HIGH for 2 minutes. Stir well, then microwave on HIGH for a further 2 minutes. Pour the sauce over the liver and onions. Cover with clingfilm and microwave on HIGH for 3 minutes. Serve immediately.

✳ Freeze for up to 6 months.

≋ Microwave on DEFROST for 6–8 minutes. Stand for 10 minutes. Cover and microwave on HIGH for 10 minutes to reheat, stirring once.

Cheese-stuffed Chicken Breasts

SERVES 4

4 chicken breasts, skinned and boned
100 g (4 oz) Emmenthal cheese, cut into 4 fingers
salt and black pepper
8 rashers streaky bacon, rinded
150 ml (¼ pint) chicken stock
5 tablespoons double cream
2 egg yolks
½ teaspoon dried dill leaves
microwave seasoning, optional

Lift out the loose fillet from the underside of each breast. Place the breasts and fillets between 2 sheets of baking parchment or clingfilm. Beat with a rolling pin to flatten. Remove the parchment or clingfilm.

Place a piece of cheese on each breast. Cover the cheese with the fillets. Dust with salt and pepper. Wrap the chicken breasts around the cheese to make parcels. Cut the bacon in half lengthways and use to wrap each, securing with wooden cocktail sticks.

Place the chicken parcels in a shallow casserole dish and add the stock. Cover and cook on HIGH for 10 minutes, turning each chicken portion halfway through. Remove the chicken and keep hot.

Whisk the cream, egg yolks and dill into the stock. Cook on HIGH for 7 minutes whisking every 2 minutes. Adjust seasoning to taste.

Sprinkle the chicken with microwave seasoning or brown under a preheated hot grill, if wished. Serve the sauce with the chicken.

✳ Freeze chicken and stock separately for 2 months.

≋ Cook from frozen for 10 minutes on DEFROST.

Above Cheese-stuffed chicken breasts

Vegetable Curry

SERVES 4

1 onion, finely chopped
225 g (8 oz) carrots, sliced
225 g (8 oz) potatoes, peeled and cubed
350 g (12 oz) cauliflower, cut into small florets
225 g (8 oz) courgettes, sliced
8 small okra, trimmed (optional)
1 red pepper, cored, seeded and cut into strips
25 g (1 oz) butter
1 teaspoon chilli powder
1½ teaspoons ground cumin
1½ teaspoons ground coriander
½ teaspoon turmeric
¼ teaspoon garlic salt
1 tablespoon tomato purée
300 ml (½ pint) vegetable stock
2 tablespoons natural yogurt
1 teaspoon lemon juice
2 tomatoes, peeled and chopped

Place the onion, carrots and potatoes in a large shallow dish with 1 tablespoon water. Cover and cook on HIGH for 10 minutes until the vegetables are tender. Leave to stand, covered.

Place the cauliflower in a shallow dish, cover and cook on HIGH for 5 minutes. Stir in the courgettes, okra if using, and red pepper and cook for a further 5 minutes. Mix with the potato, onion and carrot. Leave to stand, covered.

Place the butter in a glass jug with the spices, garlic salt and tomato purée. Mix until smooth. Blend in the stock, natural yogurt and lemon juice. Cover and cook on HIGH for 3 minutes, stirring after each minute. Stir in the tomatoes. Pour the sauce over the vegetables and stir well to mix. Cover and leave to stand.

Reheat the curry on HIGH for 3 minutes and serve immediately.

Serving suggestion: Serve on a bed of rice with a selection of chutneys, relishes and pappadoms.

✳ Freeze the curry for up to 3 months.

≈ Microwave on DEFROST for 20 minutes to thaw. Microwave on HIGH for 8–10 minutes to reheat.

Bean Pilaf

SERVES 4

1 clove garlic, crushed
1 onion, chopped
1 small red pepper, cored, seeded and cut into strips
1 small green pepper, cored, seeded and cut into strips
1 tablespoon olive oil
175 g (6 oz) long-grain rice
450 ml (¾ pint) chicken stock
1 teaspoon turmeric
salt and black pepper
6 cardamom pods, crushed
6 whole cloves
pinch of mace
25 g (1 oz) sultanas
1 × 439g (15½ oz) can red kidney beans, drained
50 g (2 oz) blanched almonds, cut into strips
25 g (1 oz) hazelnuts, chopped
25 g (1 oz) pine nuts (optional)
fresh coriander leaves, to garnish

Mix garlic, onion, peppers and oil together in a large bowl. Cover and cook on HIGH for 7–8 minutes, stirring once during cooking. Stir in the rice, stock, turmeric, salt and pepper, cardamom, cloves, mace and sultanas. Cover and cook on HIGH for 12–15 minutes, stirring once.

Add the beans. Leave to stand, covered for 15 minutes. Cook on HIGH for 5–6 minutes until piping hot. Stir in the almonds, hazelnuts and pine nuts, if using. Taste and adjust the seasoning.

Serve garnished with coriander leaves.

Note: 3 strands of saffron may be used instead of the turmeric.

Serving suggestion: Serve with a cucumber and yogurt salad.

Variation: Substitute brown rice for the long-grain rice and vegetable stock for the chicken stock.

✳ Freeze for up to 2 months.

≈ Cook from frozen on DEFROST for 6–8 minutes, breaking down the pilaf as it thaws. Allow to stand for 10 minutes. Cook on HIGH for 6 minutes to reheat, stirring once.

86

Spaghetti with Seafood Sauce

SERVES 4

1.75 litres (3 pints) boiling water

½ teaspoon salt

1 tablespoon oil

275 g (10 oz) spaghetti

1 × 397 g (14 oz) can tomatoes

1 tablespoon tomato purée

225 g (8 oz) peeled prawns, thawed if frozen

1 × 170 g (6 oz) can crabmeat, drained

1 × 170 g (6 oz) can mussels, drained

12 pimento-stuffed olives, sliced

1 teaspoon fennel seeds (optional)

salt and black pepper

TO GARNISH:
grated Parmesan cheese
6 pimento-stuffed olives, sliced

Pour the boiling water into a 2.25 litre (4 pint) heatproof mixing bowl. Add the salt and oil. Immerse the spaghetti in the hot water, curling the strands round as they soften. Cover with clingfilm, puncture, and microwave on HIGH for 8 minutes. Set aside, covered.

Place the tomatoes with their juice, the tomato purée, prawns, crabmeat, mussels, olives and fennel seeds, if using, in a large jug. Add salt and pepper to taste.

Cover with clingfilm, and puncture. Microwave on HIGH for 6 minutes, stirring once halfway through cooking.

Drain the spaghetti, arrange it on a serving dish and pour over the seafood sauce. Sprinkle liberally with Parmesan cheese, and garnish with the olive slices.

Serving suggestions: Serve with a mixed salad dressed with olive oil and lemon juice. To drink with this dish, try an Italian dry white wine such as Orvieto secco, Frascati or Lugano — a slightly fuller dry white wine.

✳ Not suitable for freezing.

Left Bean pilaf; **Right** Vegetable curry

Honey and Orange Glazed Duck

SERVES 3–4

2.5 kg (5½ lb) duck

pared rind of 1 orange and finely grated rind of 1 orange

2 tablespoons orange juice

3 tablespoons thick honey

1 tablespoon mild wholegrain mustard

½ teaspoon Worcestershire sauce

½ teaspoon paprika

salt and black pepper

TO GARNISH:
thin slices of orange
flat-leaved parsley

Wipe the duck inside and out with kitchen paper. Place the pared orange rind in the cavity and truss the bird securely.

Combine the grated orange rind and juice, honey, mustard, Worcestershire sauce, paprika, salt and pepper until evenly blended.

Place the duck on a microwave roasting rack in a deep casserole dish. Pour over the honey and orange mixture, reserving 2 tablespoons. Cover with a split roasting bag or casserole lid. Cook on HIGH for 38–55 minutes or, 7–10 minutes per 450 g (1 lb). Halfway through cooking, turn the bird breast-side down and baste thoroughly with the cooking juices.

Drain off the cooking juices. Reserve and keep warm for future use. Cover the bird completely in loose foil and allow to stand for 10–15 minutes. Test by inserting a sharp knife or skewer deep into the thigh, if the juices run clear the duck is cooked. If the juices run pink, remove the foil and return the bird to the microwave cooker and cook on HIGH for a further 5 minutes.

Meanwhile, skim off as much fat as possible from the cooking juices. Serve the juices in a warmed sauceboat. Brush the duck with the reserved honey and orange glaze before serving. Garnish with orange slices and sprigs of parsley.

✳ Freeze the duck and glaze separately for up to 2 months. To serve, allow to thaw overnight in the refrigerator and serve cold.

Creamy Scalloped Potatoes

SERVES 4

1 onion, finely sliced

450 g (1 lb) potatoes, peeled and thinly sliced

salt and black pepper

1 × 142 ml (5 fl oz) carton single cream

25 g (1 oz) butter

25 g (1 oz) Parmesan cheese, grated

Layer the onion and potatoes neatly in a shallow casserole. Sprinkle each layer with salt and pepper. Pour over the cream. Dot the butter over the top and sprinkle the Parmesan cheese over. Cover and cook on HIGH for 20–25 minutes until the potatoes are tender and have absorbed the liquid.

Variation: For a light supper dish, serve topped with crispy crumbled bacon.

✳ Not suitable for freezing.

Carrots and Celery Julienne

SERVES 4

6 celery stalks, cut into matchstick strips

225 g (8 oz) carrots, peeled and cut into matchstick strips

25 g (1 oz) butter, diced

finely grated rind of ½ lemon

½ teaspoon caster sugar

salt and black pepper

1 teaspoon chopped parsley, to garnish

Place the celery and carrots in a 900 ml (1½ pint) oval or round casserole dish. Dot with the butter. Sprinkle over the lemon rind and sugar, and season well with salt and pepper. Sprinkle over 2 tablespoons water. Cover with clingfilm and puncture.

Microwave on HIGH for 10 minutes. Stir the vegetables halfway through to ensure that they cook evenly.

Allow to stand for 5 minutes, covered. Sprinkle with parsley before serving.

✳ Not suitable for freezing.

89

Left: Top Honey and orange glazed duck; **Bottom** Carrots and celery julienne

Baked Blackcurrant Cheesecake

SERVES 6–8

50 g (2 oz) soft margarine

50 g (2 oz) caster sugar

1 egg

50 g (2 oz) self-raising flour

1 × 142 ml (5 fl oz) carton whipping cream, whipped

100 g (4 oz) frozen blackcurrants, thawed

CHEESE TOPPING:
225 g (8 oz) cream cheese, softened
225 g (8 oz) curd cheese
50 g (2 oz) caster sugar
2 eggs, beaten
1 × 142 ml (5 fl oz) carton soured cream
3 tablespoons blackcurrant jam

Beat together the margarine, sugar, egg and flour for 2 minutes until smooth. Line a 20 cm (8 inch) round deep dish with clingfilm. Spoon the mixture into the dish and spread evenly. Cook on HIGH for 3 minutes. Allow to stand while making the cheese topping.

Beat together all the ingredients except the jam, until smooth. Pour into a large bowl and cook on HIGH for 5 minutes, whisking twice during cooking. Spread the jam on the sponge base. Pour the cheese topping carefully over the top. Cook on HIGH for 5 minutes. Allow to cool, then chill. Remove from the dish and peel off the clingfilm.

Pipe a border of whipped cream round the edge of the cheesecake. Arrange the blackcurrants in the centre.

Serving suggestion: Serve on a summer afternoon with tea or a fruit punch.

Variations: Use fresh lightly cooked blackcurrants, when in season, or half a can of blackcurrant pie filling. Other fruits, such as raspberries, peaches or gooseberries may be used. Use a jam which complements the fruit selected.

* Freeze for up to 1 month before finishing with the cream and blackcurrants. To serve, thaw for 4 hours at room temperature.

≈ Microwave on DEFROST for 5–6 minutes to thaw, turning the dish twice. Allow to stand for 5–6 minutes. Decorate with the cream and blackcurrants before serving.

Courgette and Tomato Chutney

MAKES 1.75 kg (4 lb)

750 g (1½ lb) ripe tomatoes, skinned and quartered

450 g (1 lb) courgettes, chopped

2 onions, finely chopped

100 g (4 oz) sultanas

100 g (4 oz) demerara sugar

1 teaspoon allspice

1 teaspoon ginger

1 teaspoon mixed spice

1 teaspoon salt

black pepper

150 ml (¼ pint) cider vinegar

Place all the ingredients in a large dish. Cook on HIGH for 15 minutes, stirring occasionally, until the mixture thickens. Three-quarters cover the bowl with clingfilm and cook on HIGH for a further 25 minutes, stirring 3 times during cooking to prevent the surface of the chutney drying out, leave to stand for 5 minutes then pour into sterilized jars.

Cover tightly with rust proof lids or double clingfilm. Leave to mature for 1–2 months before using.

* Not suitable for freezing.

Lemon, Lime and Orange Curd

MAKES 750 g (1½ lb)

grated rind and juice of 2 lemons, 1 lime and 1 orange

350 g (12 oz) sugar

100 g (4 oz) unsalted butter, cut into pieces

4 eggs, beaten and strained

Place the rind, juice and sugar in a large dish. Cook on HIGH for about 3½ minutes, stirring 3 times, until the sugar dissolves. Stir in the butter. Cook on HIGH for 1½ minutes until completely melted. Cool slightly.

Gradually whisk in the eggs. Cook on HIGH for 5–6 minutes, whisking 3 or 4 times during cooking. Whisk steadily for about 5 minutes, until the curd thickens. Pour into warmed sterilized jars and seal.

Note: Will keep for up to 1 month in the refrigerator.

* Not suitable for freezing.

91

Blackcap Pudding with Lemon Sauce

SERVES 4

120 g (4½ oz) soft margarine

75 g (3 oz) seedless raisins

100 g (4 oz) caster sugar

2 eggs, beaten

100 g (4 oz) self-raising flour

2 tablespoons milk

finely grated rind of 1 large lemon

SAUCE:
2 tablespoons golden syrup
1 tablespoon cornflour
2 tablespoons lemon juice
150 ml (¼ pint) water
50 g (2 oz) walnuts, chopped

Grease a 900 ml (2 pint) pudding bowl with 15 g (½ oz) of the margarine. Press the raisins evenly over the whole of the inside of the bowl.

Place the remaining margarine, sugar, eggs, flour, milk and half the lemon rind in a mixing bowl. Beat thoroughly for 2 minutes until smooth and well blended. Spoon carefully into the pudding bowl, taking care not to dislodge the raisins.

Cover with pierced clingfilm. Cook on HIGH for 4 minutes. Leave to stand, covered, while making the sauce.

Place the golden syrup, cornflour, lemon juice and remaining lemon rind in a glass jug and blend until smooth. Stir in the water. Cook on HIGH for 2–3 minutes, stirring after every minute. Stir in the nuts. Turn the pudding out on to a warmed serving dish and hand the sauce separately.

✳ Freeze for up to 3 months. Reheat from frozen, covered, on HIGH for 2–3 minutes. Prepare the sauce just before serving.

Left Lemon, lime and orange curd; **Right** Courgette and tomato chutney

Florentines

MAKES 18

40 g (1½ oz) butter
50 g (2 oz) soft light brown sugar
1 tablespoon plain flour
25 g (1 oz) flaked almonds
25 g (1 oz) walnuts, chopped
25 g (1 oz) glacé cherries, chopped
1 tablespoon mixed peel
50 g (2 oz) plain chocolate, broken into pieces

Place the butter and sugar in a small glass bowl. Cook on HIGH for 1 minute, stirring twice to dissolve the sugar. Stir in the flour, nuts, cherries and peel and mix well.

Line the cooker floor or turntable with baking paper. Drop some of the mixture from a teaspoon on to the paper into 5 small heaps set in a circle. Cook on HIGH for 1–1½ minutes. Lift the paper from the cooker and place on a cool flat surface. While still hot, neaten the edges of the florentines by pressing with a knife. When the biscuits begin to cool and harden, slip them off the paper with a palette knife and cool on a wire rack.

Repeat to use the remaining mixture.

Place the chocolate in a small bowl and cook on HIGH for 1 minute. Stir until smooth. Spread this thinly over the backs of the biscuits. Allow to set.

Note: Florentines can be stored in an airtight tin for up to 1 week.

Variation: Coat the biscuits with milk chocolate.

✳ Not suitable for freezing.

Quick Creamy Chocolate Fudge

MAKES 750 g (1½ lb)

100 g (4 oz) plain chocolate, broken into pieces
100 g (4 oz) unsalted butter, cut into pieces
450 g (1 lb) icing sugar, sifted
3 tablespoons milk
1 teaspoon vanilla essence

Place all the ingredients in a large glass bowl. Cook, uncovered, on HIGH for 3 minutes until melted.

Beat together thoroughly until smooth. Pour into a greased and lined 18 cm (7 inch) square tin and chill until set. Lift the fudge out of the tin and using a sharp knife, cut the fudge into 49 pieces, each 2.5 cm (1 inch) square.

Serving suggestion: Wrap in small squares of grease-proof and tissue paper and put in a pretty box for a Christmas, birthday or Mother's day gift.

Variations: Chocolate hazelnut flavour: Stir in 50 g (2 oz) roughly chopped hazelnuts before chilling.
Chocolate-mint flavour: Replace the vanilla essence with a few drops of peppermint essence or Crème de Menthe liqueur.
Fruit flavour: Stir in 25 g (1 oz) roughly chopped glacé cherries and 25 g (1 oz) sultanas.
Mocha flavour: Replace the chocolate with 50 g (2 oz) cocoa powder and 2 teaspoons instant coffee powder blended with 1 teaspoon hot water. This makes a soft fudge, which is best kept chilled.

✳ Not suitable for freezing.

Peanut Cookies

MAKES 20

50 g (2 oz) soft margarine

50 g (2 oz) soft brown sugar

75 g (3 oz) crunchy peanut butter

50 g (2 oz) plain flour

¼ teaspoon salt

¼ teaspoon bicarbonate of soda

1 egg, beaten

½ teaspoon vanilla essence

25 g (1 oz) peanuts, toasted and chopped, to finish

Cream together the margarine, sugar and peanut butter. Sift half the flour with the salt and bicarbonate of soda and stir into the mixture. Stir the egg into the mixture, then flavour with vanilla essence. Add the remaining flour and mix to a soft dough.

Line the cooker floor or turntable with baking paper. Place walnut-sized spoonfuls of the mixture in a circle on the paper. Sprinkle each spoonful with some of the chopped peanuts.

Cook on HIGH for 45 seconds–1 minute. Leave for 1 minute to cool, then remove with a palette knife. Repeat with the remaining mixture.

Note: Store in an airtight tin for up to 7 days.

Serving suggestion: Serve with milk or a fruit drink for an after-school snack.

Variations: Use coarsely chopped cashews instead of peanuts for the topping. Coat one side of each cookie with melted chocolate, allow to set before serving.

✱ Not suitable for freezing.

Chocolate Mint Mousse

SERVES 4

175 g (6 oz) chocolate, broken into pieces

25 g (1 oz) unsalted butter, cut into pieces

2 tablespoons chocolate mint liqueur or a few drops peppermint essence

2 eggs, separated

TO DECORATE:
1 × 142 ml (5 fl oz) carton double cream, whipped
after-dinner wafer mints, cut in half
fresh mint sprigs

Place the chocolate in a large bowl and cook on HIGH for 2 minutes until just melted. Beat in the butter and liqueur or essence until thoroughly blended. Stir in the egg yolks.

Whisk the egg whites in a bowl until stiff. Beat 1 tablespoon of egg white into the chocolate mixture, then carefully fold in the remainder. Spoon the mixture into 4 glasses or ramekins and chill in the refrigerator. Decorate with piped cream, wafer mints and fresh mint sprigs.

Variation: Replace the mint liqueur with an orange liqueur such as Curaçao or Cointreau and add 1 tablespoon finely grated orange rind. Decorate with fresh orange slices or thin strips of orange peel.

✱ Not suitable for freezing.

Left Florentines; **Centre** Quick creamy chocolate fudge; **Right** Peanut cookies

93

· M E N U S ·

Planning the menu for a dinner party can be just as much fun as preparing the food—although it does take practice to compose a menu that combines the best selection of dishes and leaves you time to enjoy the company of your guests.

The key to a successful party is advance preparation; so in addition to following the menu countdown plan provided for each of the seven menus in this section, the following hints will help you turn a meal into a memorable event.

Select a menu which takes into account any of your guests' particular likes or dislikes or dietary needs, and ensure that the foods you have chosen are in season and available.

Using the menu as your guide, prepare a very detailed shopping list—there is nothing more annoying than finding that you have one ingredient missing when time is running short.

Cook as much as possible before the day; the menu countdown will explain which dishes can be cooked in advance.

Do as much washing-up as possible before the guests arrive so that the kitchen is clear and you can concentrate on the last minute preparation of dishes.

Don't forget to warm serving plates in advance.

With the help of these specially designed menus, your own flair and imagination can be given full rein and you will find entertaining at home immensely satisfying and rewarding—and so will your guests!

CHRISTENING PARTY·FOR·EIGHT

This menu includes savoury and sweet dishes which may be handed round or arranged as part of a buffet selection for your guests' enjoyment, and a centre-piece of carved gammon to enjoy with salad. Serve sparkling white wine or champagne with the cake.

Cheese and Pineapple Tarts

MAKES 16

175 g (6 oz) plain flour

pinch of salt

40 g (1½ oz) lard

40 g (1½ oz) hard margarine, diced

about 4 tablespoons iced water

FILLING:
100 g (4 oz) cream cheese
25 g (1 oz) Parmesan cheese, grated
150 ml (¼ pint) milk
2 eggs
black pepper
pinch of dry mustard
2 canned pineapple rings, drained and chopped
25 g (1 oz) Cheddar cheese, grated

TO GARNISH:
1 canned pineapple ring, drained
fresh parsley sprigs

Oven temperature: 190°C (375°F), Gas Mark 5
Sift the flour and salt into a bowl. Rub in the lard and margarine with the fingertips until the mixture resembles fine crumbs. Stir in enough water to make a firm dough. Knead until smooth. Cover with clingfilm and chill in the refrigerator for 30 minutes.

Roll the dough out thinly on a floured board and cut out sixteen 7.5 cm (3 inch) rounds.

Use the pastry rounds to line 16 tartlet tins. Prick all over with a fork; bake in the oven for 10 minutes.

Put all the ingredients for the filling, except the pineapple and Cheddar, in a bowl and beat until smooth. Divide the pineapple between the tartlets. Pour the filling over. Sprinkle a little grated Cheddar cheese over each tartlet. Return to the oven and cook for 15–20 minutes until set and golden.

Remove the tarts from the tins. Serve hot or cold. Garnish with pieces of pineapple and parsley sprigs.

✳ Not suitable for freezing.

MENU COUNTDOWN

ONE MONTH BEFORE:
Make the Christening cake.

THE WEEK BEFORE:
Decorate the Christening cake.

THE DAY BEFORE:
Prepare the sauce for the Smoked haddock croustades and leave covered in the refrigerator.
Make the filling for the Cheese and pineapple tarts and keep covered in the refrigerator.
Bake the pastry cases for the tarts.
Cook the Honey-roast gammon.
Bake the pastry for the Mocha cream puffs.

ON THE DAY:
Make a selection of salads.
Finish the Cheese and pineapple tarts.
Fill and finish the Mocha cream puffs.
Garnish the ham – leave covered until ready to serve.
Finish the Smoked haddock croustades.

95

Clockwise, from bottom
Mocha cream puffs, Honey-roast gammon, Smoked haddock croustades, Cheese and pineapple tarts

Smoked Haddock Croustades

MAKES 16

225 g (8 oz) smoked haddock, skinned and boned

300 ml (½ pint) milk

1 bay leaf

25 g (1 oz) butter

25 g (1 oz) flour

black pepper

1 teaspoon wholegrain mustard

50 g (2 oz) peeled prawns, thawed if frozen

2 tablespoons fresh chopped parsley

½ small French stick, cut into 16 thin slices

Place the haddock, milk and bay leaf in a shallow pan over moderate heat. Cover and simmer gently for 10–12 minutes or until the fish flakes easily. Remove the bay leaf. Strain the milk and reserve. Flake the fish.

Melt the butter in a pan. Stir in the flour, pepper and mustard; cook for 2 minutes. Stir in the reserved milk. Cook, stirring, until the sauce has thickened. Add the fish, half the prawns and parsley; cook for 1 minute.

Toast the bread on both sides until golden. Divide the fish mixture between the toasts and garnish with the remaining prawns, just before serving.

✳ Freeze the fish mixture without the prawns for up to 1 month. Thaw overnight in the refrigerator. Add the prawns and simmer for 1 minute.

Below Christening cake, decorated in yellow and white

Christening Cake

MAKES ONE 20 CM (8 INCH) CAKE

1 × 20 cm (8 inch) Rich fruit cake
(see recipe on page 77)

5 tablespoons apricot jam, warmed and sieved

500 g (1¼ lb) marzipan

MOULDING ICING:
450 g (1 lb) icing sugar
1 egg white, lightly beaten
1 teaspoon liquid glucose or glucose syrup
cornflour

ROYAL ICING:
2 egg whites
450 g (1 lb) icing sugar, sifted
1 teaspoon lemon juice
1 teaspoon glycerine (optional)
yellow food colouring

1 metre (1 yard) yellow ribbon, to finish

Brush the top and sides of the cake with the jam. Roll out the marzipan and use to cover the top and sides of the cake. Leave to dry for at least 48 hours. Position the cake on a 25 cm (10 inch) silver board.

To make the moulding icing, sift the icing sugar into a bowl. Add the egg white and the glucose and mix together with a wooden spoon until it develops a soft, pliable consistency. Knead until smooth.

Sprinkle the work surface with cornflour. Roll out the icing to a 25 cm (10 inch) round. Support the icing on a rolling pin and place it carefully over the cake. Press the icing on to the sides of the cake to cover it evenly. Using hands dipped in cornflour, rub the cake until smooth. Trim off excess icing and reserve.

To make the royal icing, beat the egg whites lightly, then gradually beat in half the icing sugar, using a wooden spoon. Add the lemon juice, glycerine, if using, and half the remaining sugar. Beat well until smooth and very white. Gradually beat in sufficient of the remaining icing sugar to give a consistency which will stand in soft peaks.

Place the icing in an airtight container, or cover the bowl with a damp cloth, and leave for several hours.

Cut the ribbon to fit around the cake and secure with a little royal icing.

Half fill a greaseproof paper piping bag, fitted with a star nozzle, with the royal icing. Pipe a row of stars around the base of the cake. On the top edge of the cake, pipe a row of stars a little apart and on the side of the cake, pipe a row of stars a little below to alternate with the top row. Mark a 9 cm (3½ inch) circle in the centre of the cake with a cutter and pipe stars around the circle.

Colour the remaining royal icing pale yellow and, using a small writing nozzle, pipe threads of icing diagonally from the top to the bottom row of stars at the top edge of the cake. Repeat in the opposite direction. Pipe a small bead of icing on top of each star on the top and around the base of the cake.

To make the cradle, mould a cradle base from 50 g (2 oz) moulding icing and use 25 g (1 oz) to form the hood. Attach the hood to the base so that the join is not noticeable. Use a small piece of icing to form a pillow and place in position in the cradle.

Tint 25 g (1 oz) of the moulding icing pale yellow; roll out on a board sprinkled with icing sugar. Cut out a cover for the cradle just large enough to hang over the sides. Mark a lattice pattern on the cover using a sharp knife. Lay the cover over the cradle, pinching the corners to represent fabric folds. Position the cradle on the cake using a little royal icing.

✳ Not suitable for freezing.

Honey-roast Gammon

SERVES 8

1.75 kg (4 lb) gammon joint
2 bay leaves
1 onion, quartered
1 stick celery, roughly chopped
1 carrot, sliced
2 sprigs fresh parsley
1 sprig fresh thyme
8 peppercorns

GLAZE:
2 tablespoons thick honey
2 tablespoons demerara sugar
black pepper
1 teaspoon ground cinnamon
1 tablespoon mustard seeds, crushed

TO GARNISH:
32 cloves
8 glacé cherries, quartered

Oven temperature: 180°C (350°F), Gas Mark 4

Soak the gammon joint overnight in fresh cold water.

Place it in a large saucepan of fresh cold water to cover, bring to the boil, then drain.

Return the gammon to the pan. Cover with fresh water, add the bay leaves, onion, celery, carrot, parsley, thyme and peppercorns and bring to the boil. Reduce the heat so that the water is just simmering. Remove any scum from the surface, then cover the pan and simmer for 1 hour.

Remove the gammon from the cooking liquid. When it is cool enough to handle, strip off the skin to leave the fat exposed. Using a sharp knife, slash the fat in a criss-cross pattern.

Mix all the glaze ingredients together and spread over the fat. Place the gammon in a greased roasting pan. Cover with foil and bake for 30 minutes. Remove the foil and continue to bake for a further 25 minutes, until crisp and golden.

Lift the gammon on to a serving dish and allow to cool. To garnish, pierce each cherry with a clove and stud into the joint.

✳ Freeze for up to 4 weeks. Thaw for 12 hours in the refrigerator.

≋ Microwave on DEFROST for 20 minutes. Leave to stand for 10 minutes.

Mocha Cream Puffs

MAKES 8

65 g (2½ oz) plain flour
50 g (2 oz) butter
150 ml (¼ pint) water
2 eggs, beaten

FILLING:
1 teaspoon instant coffee
100 g (4 oz) plain chocolate, melted
1 × 284 ml (10 fl oz) carton double or whipping cream, whipped

TOPPING:
50 g (2 oz) plain chocolate
15 g (½ oz) butter
1 tablespoon boiling water
1 teaspoon instant coffee

Oven temperature: 220°C (425°F), Gas Mark 7

Sift the flour on to a piece of kitchen paper. Put the butter and water in a large saucepan. Heat gently until the butter has melted then bring to boiling point. Remove from the heat and immediately pour in the flour all at once. Beat vigorously until a smooth ball of dough is formed and the sides of the pan are clean. Beat in the eggs a little at a time until the dough is firm, smooth and shiny (you may not need all of the egg).

Put the mixture into a large piping bag, fitted with a 1 cm (½ inch) plain nozzle. Pipe the mixture into 8 ball shapes, spaced well apart on a greased baking sheet. Bake for 20–25 minutes until the puffs are risen, golden and crisp. Make a slit in the side of each puff to release the steam and cool on a wire rack.

To make the filling, blend the coffee powder into the chocolate until smooth. Cool, then gently fold into the whipped cream. Split the puffs horizontally and spoon or pipe the mocha cream filling into the bases.

To make the topping, put all the ingredients in a bowl placed over a pan of hot water. Stir until melted. Dip the tops off the puffs into this mixture, then reassemble the puffs. Chill before serving.

✳ Freeze the unfilled puffs for up to 3 months. Place frozen puffs on a greased baking sheet and cook in a 160°C (325°F), Gas Mark 3 oven for 10 minutes. Cool before filling and topping.

COVERING THE CHRISTENING CAKE WITH MARZIPAN

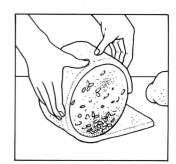

97

Brush the cake with warmed and sieved apricot jam. Roll out two-thirds of the marzipan to a strip the depth of the cake and long enough to fit around the cake. Press the marzipan on to the cake by rolling the cake on its side, as shown.

Roll-out the remaining marzipan and invert the cake on to it. Press down firmly and trim the edges. Turn the cake over and leave for at least 3 days in a cool, dry place before icing.

CHRISTMAS·DAY LUNCH·FOR·EIGHT

Start with Smoked trout creams, then serve bread sauce, carrots and sprouts with the Roast turkey with port wine sauce. Also try the Parsnip and parsley croquettes and Chestnuts with bacon. Individual Christmas puddings make a delightful finish.

MENU COUNTDOWN

AT LEAST ONE MONTH BEFORE:
Make the Individual Christmas puddings.

ON CHRISTMAS EVE:
Make the puff pastry shapes for the Smoked trout creams.
Make the stuffing for the Roast turkey with port wine sauce; cover and chill.
Make traditional accompaniments, such as bread sauce; cover and chill.
Prepare and coat the Parsnip and parsley croquettes, ready to fry.
Cook and peel the chestnuts for the Chestnuts with bacon.

ON CHRISTMAS MORNING:
Stuff the turkey and roast for 3½–4 hours.
Make the port wine sauce for the turkey.
Reheat the bread sauce.
Reheat the puddings.
Finish the Chestnuts with bacon.
Fry the Parsnip and parsley croquettes.
Boil the carrots and sprouts, keep hot.
Make the Smoked trout creams, keep warm.

Smoked Trout Creams

SERVES 8

100 g (4 oz) puff pastry, thawed if frozen

beaten egg, to glaze

15 g (½ oz) butter

1 teaspoon oil

1 shallot, finely chopped

85 ml (3 fl oz) white wine

1 × 142 ml (5 fl oz) carton double cream

salt and black pepper

pinch of cayenne pepper

1 teaspoon black peppercorns

2 smoked trout, filleted

fresh parsley sprigs, to garnish

Oven temperature: 220°C (425°F), Gas Mark 7
Roll the pastry out on a floured board to a 10 × 20 cm (4 × 8 inch) rectangle. Cut into 8 fingers each 2.5 × 10 cm (1 × 4 inch). Score with a sharp knife in a criss–cross pattern. Brush with the beaten egg and transfer to a greased baking sheet. Bake for 10–15 minutes or until risen and golden. Keep warm.

Heat the butter and oil in a frying pan and fry the shallot over a gentle heat for 4 minutes. Add the wine, cream, salt and pepper, cayenne and peppercorns and simmer for 5 minutes until reduced and thickened.

Cut each of the trout fillets in half and lay them in the sauce and simmer for a further 3 minutes until warmed through. Arrange a piece of trout in sauce and a piece of flaky pastry on each warmed plate. Garnish with parsley and serve immediately.

Variation: Substitute smoked mackerel for smoked trout.

✴ Freeze in a rigid container for 1 month. To serve, cook in a 190°C (375°F), Gas Mark 5 oven for 5–10 minutes.

Roast Turkey with Port Wine Sauce

SERVES 8

4½–5½ kg (10–12 lb) oven-ready turkey, washed and dried, inside and out, with kitchen paper

50 g (2 oz) butter

4 rashers streaky bacon

fresh parsley sprigs, to garnish

STUFFING:
450 g (1 lb) pork sausage meat
100 g (4 oz) streaky bacon, rinded and chopped
100 g (4 oz) fresh white breadcrumbs
1 onion, finely chopped
1 red pepper, cored, seeded and diced
1 teaspoon dried mixed herbs
finely grated rind of ½ lemon
salt and black pepper

SAUCE:
1 tablespoon plain flour
salt and black pepper
150 ml (¼ pint) port
450 ml (¾ pint) turkey giblet stock
2 tablespoons redcurrant jelly

Oven temperature: 180°C (350°F), Gas Mark 4
First make the stuffing. Place all the ingredients in a large bowl and blend together until evenly mixed. Use to stuff the neck end of the turkey, pressing in firmly. Replace the neck flap and secure with a skewer or sew with a needle and coarse thread.

Place the bird on a trivet in a large roasting pan. Spread the skin well with the butter and lay the bacon over the breast. Cover loosely with foil. Roast for 3 hours, basting twice. Remove the foil and continue to cook for another 30–45 minutes, basting frequently.

To test, insert a skewer deep into the thigh meat. If the juices run clear the bird is ready, if they are pink, return to the oven for a further 15 minutes, then test again. Remove the turkey to a warmed serving platter. Cover loosely with foil and allow to stand while making the sauce.

Skim all but one tablespoon of fat from the roasting pan. Place the pan on the hob over gentle heat. Stir in the flour. Add salt and pepper. Cook for 2 minutes, stirring and scraping the meat residues off the bottom of the pan. Gradually blend in the port and stock. Add the redcurrant jelly. Cook, stirring, for 5 minutes. Strain into a gravy boat.

Garnish the turkey with parsley and serve with the port wine sauce.

Note: To make turkey giblet stock, cover giblets with a pint of cold water. Add half an onion, bouquet garni and seasoning, then simmer gently for 1 hour. Strain before using.

✴ Not suitable for freezing.

Parsnip and Parsley Croquettes

SERVES 8

1 kg (2 lb) parsnips, peeled, cored and sliced
25 g (1 oz) butter
3 tablespoons fresh chopped parsley
pinch of nutmeg
salt and black pepper
flour, for coating
1 egg, beaten with 1 tablespoon water
100 g (4 oz) dry white breadcrumbs
oil, for deep frying

Put the parsnips in a saucepan of boiling salted water and boil for 5–10 minutes or until tender. Drain and mash thoroughly. Stir in the butter, parsley, nutmeg, salt and pepper. When cool put the parsnips in a bowl, cover and refrigerate for 2 hours.

Using well floured hands, shape the mashed parsnips into small cylinders. Coat in the beaten egg then in the breadcrumbs.

Heat the oil to 180°C–190°C (350°F–375°F) or until a cube of stale bread browns in 30 seconds. Add the parsnip croquettes in batches and fry for 8–10 minutes until golden brown. Remove with a slotted spoon and drain on kitchen paper.

✳ Not suitable for freezing.

Chestnuts with Bacon

SERVES 8

750 g (1½ lb) chestnuts
chicken or vegetable stock
25 g (1 oz) butter
1 onion, sliced
4 rashers back bacon, rinded and cut into strips
salt and black pepper
1 × 142 ml (5 fl oz) carton double cream
1 tablespoon snipped chives

Pierce the chestnut shells with a sharp knife. Place in a pan with enough stock to cover. Bring to the boil, cover and cook for 40 minutes until the nuts are soft. Drain and allow to cool slightly then peel off the shell and inner membrane.

Melt the butter in a frying pan. Add the onion and bacon and cook over moderate heat for 5 minutes. Add salt and pepper, chestnuts and cream. Simmer gently for 5 minutes. Stir in the chives. Serve hot.

Note: The peeled chestnuts can be covered and refrigerated for up to one day in advance.

Variation: When fresh chestnuts are not in season, use canned chestnuts.

✳ Not suitable for freezing.

Individual Christmas Puddings

SERVES 8

175 g (6 oz) currants

175 g (6 oz) raisins

100 g (4 oz) sultanas

finely grated rind of 1 orange

finely grated rind of 1 lemon

175 g (6 oz) fresh white breadcrumbs

50 g (2 oz) plain flour

25 g (1 oz) blanched almonds, chopped

25 g (1 oz) walnuts, chopped

pinch of ground nutmeg

pinch of ground cinnamon

½ teaspoon mixed spice

50 g (2 oz) soft dark brown sugar

25 g (1 oz) chopped mixed peel

2 eggs, beaten

4 tablespoons sherry or brandy

85 ml (3 fl oz) milk

100 g (4 oz) butter, melted

TO DECORATE:
tiny holly sprigs
icing sugar

In a large bowl place the fruit, orange and lemon rinds, breadcrumbs, flour, nuts, spices, sugar and peel. Stir well to mix. Beat together the eggs, sherry or brandy, milk and butter. Blend the two mixtures together. Press into 8 greased dariole moulds, rame-kin dishes or cups. Cover each pudding with a circle of greased greaseproof paper and a double thickness of foil; fold a pleat in the centre of each piece of foil to allow for expansion. Tie with string; stand overnight.

Use a steamer or put the puddings in 1 or 2 large saucepans and pour in enough boiling water to come halfway up the sides of the moulds. Cover the pans and steam for 4 hours. Add more water as necessary to keep the level constant.

Cover the puddings with fresh greaseproof paper and foil. Store in a cool dry place for up to 1 year.

To reheat, steam for 1½ hours. Remove wrappings and turn out on to individual serving plates. Decorate each with holly; dust with icing sugar and serve.

Serving suggestion: Serve with brandy butter.

✱ These puddings will keep well without freezing.

≈ To reheat the puddings, remove the foil, cover with clingfilm and cook on HIGH for 5 minutes.

ST·VALENTINE'S ·DINNER·

This is a very special menu with delicate and unusual dishes. Lightly poached Salmon quenelles complement the more robust Duck breasts in piquant fruit sauce. A pretty dessert of Passion fruit heartcakes will finish the romantic meal perfectly.

Salmon Quenelles

SERVES 2

100 g (4 oz) fresh, skinned, boned salmon

1 egg white

4 tablespoons double cream

pinch of cayenne pepper

salt and black pepper

fresh chervil, or coriander sprigs, to garnish

SAUCE:
1 tablespoon tarragon vinegar
6 black peppercorns
1 egg yolk
pinch of white pepper
50 g (2 oz) unsalted butter,
1 teaspoon chopped fresh tarragon

Sieve the fish or place in a blender or food processor and blend until smooth. Stir in the egg white and rub through a fine sieve into a bowl. Cover with clingfilm and chill for 2 hours in the refrigerator.

Set the bowl in a container of crushed ice. Gradually beat in the cream, cayenne, salt and pepper. Using 2 tablespoons, shape the quenelles into slender ovals. Place the quenelles carefully in an oiled frying pan. Gently pour in just enough hot water to cover the quenelles. Place the frying pan on the hob and heat gently to just below boiling. Poach the quenelles for 10 minutes, turning half-way through cooking. Remove from the heat but leave the quenelles in the hot water for 10 minutes.

Put the vinegar and peppercorns in a small saucepan over high heat and boil rapidly until only 1 teaspoonful remains. Place the egg yolk in a heat-proof bowl and strain the vinegar into it. Season with pepper. Place the bowl over a pan of sim-mering water and whisk continuously until thick and creamy. Remove from the heat and very gradually whisk in the butter until the sauce is thick and glossy. Fold in the tarragon. Drain the quenelles; Serve on warm plates with the sauce and garnish.

✱ Not suitable for freezing.

Duck Breasts in Piquant Fruit Sauce

SERVES 2

2 duck breasts, skinned and boned

salt and black pepper

15 g (½ oz) butter

1 tablespoon oil

SAUCE:
85 ml (3 fl oz) red wine
150 ml (¼ pint) chicken or duck stock
100 g (4 oz) frozen raspberries, thawed
100 g (4 oz) frozen redcurrants, thawed
4 whole allspice berries, crushed

Season the duck breasts, place on a board and cover with clingfilm. Beat with a rolling pin to flatten.

Heat the butter and oil in a frying pan over moderate heat. Add the duck breasts and fry for 10–15 minutes on each side. Drain and keep hot.

Pour off most of the fat from the pan. Add the wine, stock, fruits, allspice and a little freshly ground pepper. Bring to the boil and cook over high heat for 4 minutes until the sauce has reduced and thickened slightly. Rub the sauce through a sieve. Return to the pan and reheat gently. Adjust seasoning to taste.

Carve the duck breasts into thin slices. Arrange on serving plates and pour the sauce over.

✳ Freeze the cooked breasts and sauce separately for up to 4 months. To serve, thaw overnight in the refrigerator and reheat, covered, in a preheated oven at 180°C (350°F), Gas Mark 4 for 20–25 minutes.

≋ Microwave together on DEFROST for 20–25 minutes, stirring the sauce twice to thaw. Microwave on HIGH for 2–3 minutes to reheat.

Passion Fruit Heartcakes

SERVES 2

75 g (3 oz) plain flour, sifted

50 g (2 oz) butter

25 g (1 oz) caster sugar

½ teaspoon almond essence

icing sugar, to finish

FILLING:
1 × 142 ml (5 fl oz) carton double or whipping cream
1 teaspoon vanilla essence
1 tablespoon caster sugar
2 passion fruits, halved

101

Oven temperature: 180°C (350°F), Gas Mark 4
Grease a baking sheet and line it with greased greaseproof paper.

Put the flour, butter, sugar and almond essence in a mixing bowl and rub together with the fingertips until the mixture begins to come together. Knead to a firm ball with the hands. Roll out on a floured surface and cut out 4 × 7.5 cm (3 inch) heart shapes. Place on the baking sheet and bake for 15–20 minutes until lightly browned. Cool on the baking sheet for 10 minutes, then transfer to a wire rack.

To make the filling, place the cream, vanilla essence and sugar in a large bowl and whisk together until soft peaks form. Place in a piping bag, fitted with a medium-size star nozzle. Pipe cream around the edge of each heart-shaped biscuit. Scoop the pulp from each passion fruit and use to fill the centre of each heartcake. Dust with a little icing sugar before serving.

✳ Not suitable for freezing. Store the heart-shaped biscuits in an airtight tin for up to one week.

Above Salmon quenelles, with tarragon butter sauce

MENU COUNTDOWN

THE DAY BEFORE:
Make the biscuits for the Passion fruit heartcakes.

THE MORNING BEFORE:
Make and shape the Salmon quenelles.
Prepare the Duck breasts in piquant fruit sauce and chill.

BEFORE SERVING:
Finish the heartcakes and chill.
Poach the quenelles and make the tarragon sauce. Keep warm.
Cook the duck breasts and sauce; keep hot.

SPECIAL·DINNER PARTY·FOR·SIX

For a special occasion it's fun to introduce unusual items into the menu to surprise and impress your guests. Follow the Menu Countdown to prepare in advance so you can relax with your guests before the meal.

MENU COUNTDOWN

THE DAY BEFORE:
Make the Iced zabaglione cake.
Make the tomato sauce for the Spinach timbales.

THE MORNING BEFORE:
Prepare the vegetables for the Mange-tout peas and carrots julienne and the Celeriac au gratin: wrap in polythene bags and refrigerate.
Prepare the Trout in puff pastry lattice.

BEFORE SERVING:
Cook the Spinach timbales and reheat the tomato sauce.
Bake the Trout in puff pastry lattice.
Cook the Celeriac au gratin.
Cook the Mange-tout peas and carrots julienne.

102

Spinach Timbales with Tomato Sauce

SERVES 6

225 g (8 oz) frozen leaf spinach, thawed

25 g (1 oz) butter

6 spring onions, trimmed and chopped

2 tablespoons flour

300 ml (½ pint) milk

salt and black pepper

pinch of mace

8 egg yolks

8 tablespoons double cream

TOMATO SAUCE:
2 tablespoons olive oil
½ small onion, finely chopped
1 × 397 g (14 oz) can chopped tomatoes
1 tablespoon fresh chopped basil
1 teaspoon dried oregano

Oven temperature: 180°C (350°F), Gas Mark 4
Use a few spinach leaves to line 6 buttered ramekin dishes. Chop the remainder and squeeze dry.

Melt the butter in a small saucepan over moderate heat. Add the spring onions and cook for 2 minutes. Stir in the flour and cook for 1 minute. Gradually add the milk and cook, stirring, until thickened. Add salt, pepper and mace. Beat in the egg yolks, cream and spinach. Pour into ramekins.

Put the ramekins in a roasting pan and pour in enough boiling water to come halfway up the sides. Bake for 35–40 minutes or until firm.

Meanwhile, make the sauce. Heat the oil in a small pan. Add the onion and fry for 2 minutes. Stir in the remaining ingredients. Simmer gently, stirring occasionally, for 10 minutes or until reduced. Sieve the sauce or pour into a blender or food processor and blend until smooth. Carefully turn out the timbales on to small plates; serve with the sauce.

✱ Not suitable for freezing.

Trout in Puff Pastry Lattice

SERVES 6

6 small fresh trout, trimmed and washed

6 bay leaves

pared rind of ½ lemon, finely chopped

75 g (3 oz) butter

salt and black pepper

750 g (1½ lb) puff pastry, thawed if frozen

1 egg, beaten

2 tablespoons sesame seeds (optional)

sprigs of fresh dill, to garnish

Oven temperature: 200°C (400°F), Gas Mark 6
Place a bay leaf, some lemon rind and 15 g (½ oz) butter inside each fish. Season with salt and pepper.

Divide the pastry into 6 pieces. Roll each piece to the length of the fish and 3 times the width. Lay a fish lengthways down a piece of pastry. Cut the pastry either side of the fish into 1 cm (½ inch) strips. Bring the strips up over the fish, one by one from alternate sides plaiting on top to enclose the fish in pastry. Repeat with each remaining fish.

Place the fish on greased baking sheets. Brush the pastry with the beaten egg and sprinkle with the sesame seeds, if using. Bake for 30 minutes or until the pastry is golden and the fish tender. Carefully remove from the baking sheet. Garnish with dill.

✱ Not suitable for freezing.

Mange-tout Peas and Carrots Julienne

SERVES 6

225 g (8 oz) carrots, peeled and cut into thin sticks

1 teaspoon caster sugar

salt and black pepper

225 g (8 oz) mange-tout peas, trimmed

15 g (½ oz) butter, melted

fresh chopped parsley, to garnish

Place the carrots, sugar and seasoning in a saucepan with water to cover. Cover and simmer gently for 5 minutes.

Uncover the pan, add the mange-tout peas, and boil rapidly for 3–4 minutes until the water has reduced to a syrupy glaze and the mange-tout peas are tender but still crisp. Toss with butter and parsley.

✱ Not suitable for freezing.

Celeriac au Gratin

SERVES 6

750 g (1½ lb) celeriac, peeled and sliced

40 g (1½ oz) butter

40 g (1½ oz) flour

150 ml (¼ pint) milk

1 × 142 ml (5 fl oz) carton single cream

salt and black pepper

pinch of ground nutmeg

100 g (4 oz) mature Cheddar cheese, grated

25 g (1 oz) fresh white breadcrumbs

paprika, to garnish

Boil the celeriac in a large saucepan of salted water for 40 minutes, until tender. Drain. Layer the slices in a warm, shallow casserole dish and keep hot.

Melt the butter in a saucepan over moderate heat. Stir in the flour and cook for 1 minute. Gradually beat in the milk, cream, salt, pepper and nutmeg. Cook, stirring constantly, for 3 minutes or until thick, smooth and glossy. Add 75 g (3 oz) of the cheese and stir until melted.

Pour the sauce over the celeriac. Mix the remaining cheese with the breadcrumbs and sprinkle evenly over the celeriac. Place under a preheated grill to brown. Dust with the paprika before serving.

Variations: Replace the celeriac with cooked fennel, leeks, celery or whole baby turnips, when in season. Use Gruyère cheese instead of the Cheddar.

✴ Not suitable for freezing.

Iced Zabaglione Cake

SERVES 6

25 g (1 oz) butter, softened

25 g (1 oz) caster sugar

½ egg, beaten

25 g (1 oz) self-raising flour

½ teaspoon vanilla essence

2 tablespoons Marsala or sweet sherry

ZABAGLIONE:
8 egg yolks
75 g (3 oz) caster sugar
6 tablespoons Marsala or sweet sherry
finely grated rind of 1 lemon

Oven temperature: 190°C (375°F), Gas Mark 5
Grease and line an 18 cm (7 inch) spring-form cake tin with greased greaseproof paper. Place all the ingredients except the Marsala or sherry in a bowl; beat

for 2 minutes until smooth and spread in the tin. Bake for 15 minutes or until risen and golden.

Leave the sponge to cool in the tin. When cool sprinkle with the Marsala or sherry. Cover and place in the freezer, or the ice-making compartment of the refrigerator turned to its lowest setting.

To make the zabaglione, put the egg yolks, sugar and Marsala or sherry into a wide bowl, set over a pan of barely simmering water. Whisk the mixture continuously until it trebles in volume and becomes thick and creamy. Remove the bowl from the heat and continue to whisk gently until cold.

Stir in the lemon rind and pour the zabaglione on to the sponge base in the tin. Cover and chill for at least 3 hours.

To serve, remove the tin and paper and put the dessert on a plate. Serve at once, cut like a cake.

✴ Freeze, well wrapped, for 2–3 weeks.

Above Trout in puff pastry lattice served with Mange-tout peas and carrots julienne

103

VEGETARIAN DINNER·FOR·FOUR

A sophisticated yet simple dinner which is sure to please vegetarians and non-vegetarians alike. Serve the creamy starter with wholemeal Melba toast and offer sautéed potatoes or Hot herb bread (page 83) with the main course.

Peppered Blue Cheese with Melba Toast

SERVES 4

75 g (3 oz) unsalted butter, melted

225 g (8 oz) soft blue cheese, such as Cambazola, Gorgonzola or Dolcelatte, rind removed

175 g (6 oz) cream cheese, softened

2 teaspoons green peppercorns, drained and chopped

1 tablespoon dry sherry

black pepper

3 slices wholemeal bread

Place one-third of the melted butter in a large bowl. Beat in the cheeses, half the peppercorns, and the sherry and pepper until the mixture is creamy.

Divide the mixture between 4 small ramekin dishes and chill for one hour. Pour the remaining butter over the mixture to seal the tops.

Lightly toast the bread on both sides. Cut off the crusts using a sharp knife. Carefully split the pieces of toast horizontally through the untoasted centres. Place, untoasted sides up, briefly under the grill until the toast begins to curl. Be careful not to let the toast burn.

Garnish the with the remaining peppercorns; serve with the Melba toast.

Note: The Melba toast can be stored in an airtight container for 1–2 days. Refresh under a preheated hot grill for a few seconds before serving.

✳ Freeze for up to 2 months. Thaw for 3–4 hours at room temperature or overnight in the refrigerator.

Peas with Lettuce and Onions

SERVES 4

1 kg (2 lb) fresh green peas, shelled

50 g (2 oz) butter

1 bunch spring onions, sliced

½ Iceberg lettuce, shredded

2 sprigs fresh mint

1 teaspoon caster sugar

salt and black pepper

fresh mint sprigs, to garnish

Cook the peas in boiling salted water until just tender. Drain.

Melt the butter in a large saucepan. Stir in the onions and fry gently for 2 minutes. Stir in the lettuce, peas and mint. Cook, covered, for 2 minutes. Stir in the sugar, salt and pepper. Remove the cooked mint sprigs, garnish with fresh mint sprigs, and serve immediately.

Variation: 350 g (12 oz) frozen peas can be substituted for the fresh peas. Omit the precooking of the peas and add them with the lettuce. Cook for 5–8 minutes or until the peas are hot.

✳ Not suitable for freezing.

Below Mushroom and garlic crêpes and Peas with lettuce and onions

Mushroom and Garlic Crêpes

SERVES 4

100 g (4 oz) plain flour

salt and black pepper

pinch of dry mustard

1 egg

300 ml (½ pint) milk

25 g (1 oz) butter, melted

oil, for frying

FILLING:
50 g (2 oz) butter
1 clove garlic, crushed
2 onions, finely chopped
225 g (8 oz) button mushrooms, chopped
4 tablespoons red wine
4 tablespoons chopped fresh parsley
salt and black pepper
4 hard-boiled eggs, chopped

Place all the ingredients for the crêpes into a blender or food processor. Blend for 30 seconds until smooth. Or, place the dry ingredients in a large bowl. Make a well in the centre and put in the egg and half the milk. Whisk, gradually incorporating the flour. Then beat thoroughly until smooth. Whisk in the remaining milk and melted butter a little at a time.

Brush a heavy-based 15–20 cm (6–8 inch) frying pan with oil. Place over a moderate heat for 1 minute. Pour in just enough batter (about 2 tablespoons) to cover the base of the pan thinly. Tilt the pan so that the batter covers the base evenly. Cook for 1½ minutes until the underside is golden. Turn with a spatula and cook the other side for about 30 seconds. Turn the crêpe out on to a plate; keep warm. Repeat with remaining batter to make about 10 crêpes.

To make the filling, melt the butter in a frying pan over moderate heat. Add the garlic and onions and fry gently for 5 minutes. Add the mushrooms, red wine, parsley, salt and pepper. Fry, stirring, for a further 5 minutes. Finally, stir in the chopped eggs. Remove from the heat. Divide the filling equally between the crêpes. Fold neatly into quarters and lay on a warmed serving platter.

Variation: Make the crêpes using wholemeal flour and 3 extra tablespoons of milk.

✳ Freeze for up to 2 months. Reheat between 2 plates over simmering water or bake from frozen in a 200°C (400°F), Gas Mark 6 oven for 30 minutes.

≈ Microwave on HIGH for 3–4 minutes. Leave to stand, covered, for 5 minutes. If necessary, microwave on HIGH for a further 1–2 minutes.

Above Kiwi fruit sorbet, served with wafers

Kiwi Fruit Sorbet

SERVES 6

100 g (4 oz) caster sugar

300 ml (½ pint) water

1 tablespoon lemon juice

4 kiwi fruit, peeled halved and cored

2 egg whites

fresh lemon balm sprigs, to garnish

Place the sugar and water in a small saucepan over moderate heat. Stir to dissolve the sugar. Bring to the boil and boil gently for 10 minutes. Stir in the lemon juice and set the syrup aside to cool.

Sieve the kiwi fruit or place in a blender or food processor and blend until smooth. Mix into the cooled syrup. Pour the mixture into a container, cover and freeze to a mushy consistency (either in a freezer or in the ice-making compartment of the refrigerator, turned to its lowest setting).

Turn the mixture into a large bowl and beat until smooth. Whisk the egg whites until stiff. Beat a spoonful of egg white into the semi-frozen mixture. Carefully fold the remaining egg whites through the fruit mixture. Return to the container and freeze.

Ten minutes before serving transfer the sorbet to the refrigerator. Serve on chilled dishes garnished with sprigs of fresh lemon balm.

✳ Freeze for up to 2 months.

MENU COUNTDOWN

THE DAY BEFORE:
Make the Peppered blue cheese and the melba toast.
Make the crêpes and leave, covered, in the refrigerator.
Make the Kiwi fruit sorbet.

THE MORNING BEFORE:
Garnish the Peppered blue cheese.

BEFORE SERVING:
Refresh the melba toast.
Make the filling for the Mushroom and garlic crêpes and fill the crêpes. Keep hot.
Cook the Peas with lettuce and onions.
Allow the Kiwi fruit sorbet to soften in the refrigerator during the main course of the meal.

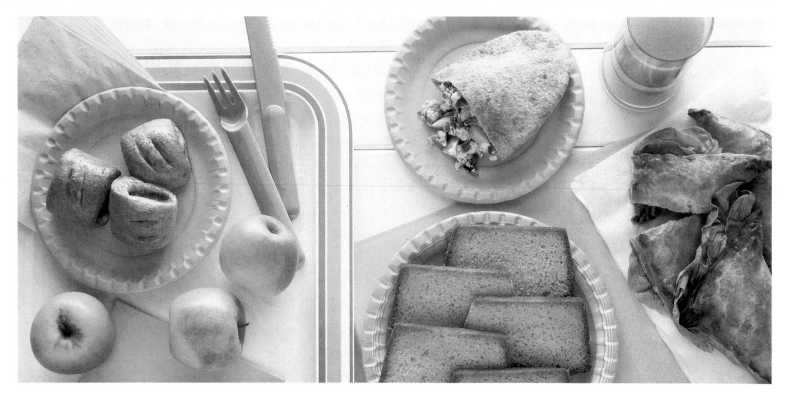

Clockwise from top: Filled pitta, stuffed with apple and blue cheese, Tomato bacon turnovers, Crystallized lemon and orange loaf and Country sausage bites

MENU COUNTDOWN

1–3 MONTHS BEFORE:
Make Country sausage bites and freeze.
Make Tomato bacon turnovers and freeze.
Make Crystallized lemon and orange loaf and freeze.

THE DAY BEFORE:
Butter the pitta breads, wrap in polythene bags and refrigerate.
Make the fillings for the pitta breads.
Make a salad but keep the dressing separate.

ON THE DAY:
Fill the pitta breads.
Combine the salad and dressing.
Pack the food and fill a flask with a hot or cold drink.

FAMILY·PICNIC·FOR FOUR

Most of the food for this picnic can be frozen ready for you to take advantage of unexpected good weather. Make a salad to balance out the meal and take plenty of paper napkins to wipe sticky fingers and a knife to cut the Crystallized lemon and orange loaf.

Country Sausage Bites

MAKES 16

150 g (5 oz) strong plain white flour

75 g (3 oz) wholemeal flour

10 g (¼ oz) fresh yeast

150 ml (¼ pint) tepid water

½ teaspoon caster sugar

½ teaspoon salt

1 egg, beaten

FILLING:
450 g (1 lb) pork sausage meat
1 teaspoon tomato purée
1 teaspoon dried mixed herbs
black pepper

Oven temperature: 220°C (425°F), Gas Mark 7

Sift the flours into a large, warmed mixing bowl. Blend the yeast with the water to a smooth cream. Add to the flour with the sugar and salt. Mix to a dough. Knead for 10 minutes until silky and elastic. Place in an oiled polythene bag and leave in a warm place for 1 hour or until doubled in size.

To make the filling, mix together all the ingredients. Using well floured hands, form the mixture into 2 long sausage shapes, 2 cm (¾ inch) in diameter.

Remove the dough from the bag and knead until smooth again. Divide the dough in half and roll each piece into a strip a little longer than the sausage shapes and 4 times as wide; brush the edges with egg. Place a sausage of filling on each and roll the dough around the filling. Seal the edges by pressing firmly together. Brush with egg and slash across the top of the rolls at regular intervals. Cut each roll into 8 pieces. Place on greased baking sheets. Cover with oiled clingfilm and leave to rise in a warm place for 40 minutes.

Remove the clingfilm and bake the sausage rolls for 20–25 minutes. Cool on a wire rack.

Variation: Use half a 275 g (10 oz) packet of brown bread mix and make up according to the manufacturer's instructions. Or, replace the fresh yeast with 1 teaspoon easy-blend dried yeast and blend into the flour before mixing the dough.

✳ Freeze for up to 1 month. To serve, thaw overnight in the refrigerator or at room temperature.

≈ Microwave on DEFROST for 4–6 minutes. Leave to stand for 10 minutes.

Filled Pittas

SERVES 4

4 fresh pitta breads, each cut across widthways to make two pockets, buttered

FILLINGS:

Chicken and Grape: Mix together 350 g (12 oz) chopped, cold, cooked chicken, 100 g (4 oz) halved, seeded green grapes, 1 teaspoon lemon juice, salt and black pepper, pinch of cayenne pepper and 4 tablespoons mayonnaise. Use to stuff pitta pockets.

Apple and blue cheese: Combine 175 g (6 oz) crumbled blue cheese, 3 bacon rashers, crisply cooked and crumbled, 2 apples, cored and chopped, 1 teaspoon lemon juice and 25 g (1 oz) chopped hazelnuts. Stir in 2 tablespoons thick natural yogurt and season with black pepper. Use to fill pitta breads.

Pork loaf: Mix together 350 g (12 oz) sausage meat, 2 tablespoons tomato ketchup, 1 tablespoon chutney, 1 egg, a few drops Worcestershire sauce, salt and black pepper. Press into a 450 g (1 lb) loaf tin, cover with foil and bake at 180°C (350°F) for 1 hour. Cool in the tin. Turn out and fill pittas with slices of pork loaf and sliced tomato.

Spicy egg mayonnaise: Fry ½ teaspoon mild curry powder and 1 chopped spring onion in 15 g (½ oz) butter for 2 minutes. Allow to cool then stir in 4 chopped hard-boiled eggs and 3 tablespoons mayonnaise. Add salt, black pepper and a few drops of Tabasco sauce to taste. Serve in pitta pockets.

✳ Freeze the Pork loaf for up to 2 months. Thaw overnight in the refrigerator. Make the remaining fillings on the day or the day before.

≈ To thaw the Pork loaf, microwave on DEFROST for 8–10 minutes. Leave to stand for 10 minutes.

Tomato Bacon Turnovers

MAKES 4

25 g (1 oz) butter

1 onion, finely chopped

175 g (6 oz) back bacon, rinded and chopped

225 g (8 oz) tomatoes, skinned, seeded and chopped

1 tablespoon chopped parsley

1 tablespoon tomato purée

black pepper

225 g (8 oz) puff pastry, thawed if frozen

1 egg, beaten

Oven temperature: 220°C (425°F), Gas Mark 7

Melt the butter in a frying pan over moderate heat. Add the onion and bacon and fry, stirring, for 4 minutes. Add the tomatoes, parsley, tomato purée and pepper. Cook, stirring, for 5 minutes or until thickened. Set aside to cool.

On a floured board, roll the pastry to a 25 cm (10 inch) square. Cut into 4 equal squares and dampen the edges with egg. Divide the bacon filling between the squares. Fold over each square on the diagonal to give triangle-shaped turnovers. Press the edges to seal.

Brush the turnovers with beaten egg and place on a greased baking sheet. Bake for 20–25 minutes until risen and golden. Cool on a wire rack.

Variation: Use 175 g (6 oz) chopped cooked ham in place of the bacon.

✳ Freeze for up to 3 months. To serve, thaw for 3 hours at room temperature.

Crystallized Lemon and Orange Loaf

MAKES A 25 CM (10 INCH) LOAF

225 g (8 oz) caster sugar

175 g (6 oz) soft margarine

3 eggs, beaten

175 g (6 oz) self-raising flour

4 tablespoons milk

grated rind and juice of ½ lemon

grated rind and juice of ½ orange

50 g (2 oz) icing sugar

Oven temperature: 180°C (350°F), Gas Mark 4

Grease and line with greased greaseproof paper a 1 kg (2 lb) loaf tin.

Place 175 g (6 oz) of the sugar, the margarine, eggs, flour, milk and lemon and orange rind in a large bowl. Beat thoroughly for 2 minutes until smooth. Turn into the loaf tin. Bake for 55–60 minutes or until golden and springy to the touch or when a skewer inserted into the centre comes out clean. Cool in the tin for 10 minutes.

Mix the fruit juices with the remaining caster sugar, and the icing sugar. Prick the surface of the cake all over with a skewer. Pour the sugar mixture evenly over the cake and allow it to soak in.

When the cake is completely cold, carefully remove from the tin.

✳ Freeze for up to 3 months. To serve, thaw at room temperature for 3 hours.

≈ Microwave on DEFROST for 4–5 minutes. Allow to stand for 10 minutes.

INFORMAL·SUPPER PARTY·FOR·FOUR

An evening with good friends is made even more relaxed and enjoyable with food that is fun to eat. The dishes in this menu can all be eaten without knives and forks, so provide finger bowls with a slice of lemon or lime and plenty of paper napkins for each guest.

MENU COUNTDOWN

THE DAY BEFORE:
Make the Bitter coffee caramels and refrigerate.
Make the spicy dip for the Chicken goujons, cover and chill.

THE MORNING BEFORE:
Make the Barbecue sauce.
Make the Black bean sauce.
Coat the Chicken goujons, chill.
Prepare a salad.

BEFORE SERVING:
Fry the Chicken goujons.
Cook the Sesame spareribs.
Reheat the Barbecue and Black bean sauces.
Turn out the Bitter coffee caramels and decorate.

108

Chicken Goujons with Spicy Dip

SERVES 4

little flour

salt and black pepper

1 egg, beaten with 1 tablespoon water

100 g (4 oz) dry white breadcrumbs

4 chicken breasts, skinned, boned and cut into long strips

oil, for deep frying

lemon wedges, to garnish

DIP:
*1 × 142 ml (5 fl oz) carton soured cream
100 g (4 oz) low-fat soft cheese
2 teaspoons snipped chives
few drops Tabasco sauce
2 tablespoons mango chutney, finely chopped*

First make the dip. Beat all the ingredients together until evenly blended. Season to taste. Spoon into a serving bowl and chill before serving.

Mix the flour with salt and pepper on a plate. Have the beaten egg ready on another plate and the breadcrumbs on a third. Toss the chicken strips in the flour to coat evenly. Next dip the chicken in the beaten egg and finally coat the pieces in breadcrumbs. Allow to chill for 10 minutes.

Heat the oil to 180°–190°C (350°–375°F) or until a cube of stale bread browns in 30 seconds. Fry the chicken pieces, in batches, for 5 minutes until golden and tender. Drain on kitchen paper.

Serve the chicken goujons hot or cold on a platter with the bowl of dip in the centre. Garnish with lemon wedges.

Note: The dip can be stored, covered, in the refrigerator for up to 24 hours.

Variation: Substitute turkey, scampi or firm white fish for the chicken.

✳ Not suitable for freezing.

Sesame Spareribs

SERVES 4

1.25 kg (2½ lb) pork spareribs

2 tablespoons oil

6 tablespoons sesame seeds

black pepper

Oven temperature: 180°C (350°F), Gas Mark 4
Separate the meat into single ribs. Brush them with oil, then sprinkle with sesame seeds and pepper. Place under a preheated hot grill and cook for 10 minutes until they are browned, turning several times during grilling. Baste frequently with the juices.

Place the ribs in a single layer in a large roasting pan. Roast for 40 minutes, basting frequently. Serve the ribs hot with Barbecue or Black bean sauce.

✳ Not suitable for freezing.

Barbecue Sauce

SERVES 4

4 tablespoons clear honey

4 tablespoons light soy sauce

3 tablespoons tomato purée

1 clove garlic, crushed

1 tablespoon mild wholegrain mustard

pinch of cayenne pepper

¼ teaspoon paprika

few drops Tabasco sauce

1 teaspoon Worcestershire sauce

salt and black pepper

2 tablespoons red wine vinegar

1 teaspoon soft brown sugar

3 tablespoons orange juice

Mix all the ingredients together in a small saucepan. Bring to the boil, stirring, over moderate heat. Lower the heat; simmer gently for 30 minutes until syrupy.

Serve hot with the sesame spareribs.

✳ Freeze for up to 2 months. To serve, thaw gently in a pan over low heat.

≈ Microwave on HIGH for 5–7 minutes, stirring frequently to thaw and reheat.

Black Bean Sauce

SERVES 4

1½ tablespoons salted black beans, soaked in water for 30 minutes

salt and black pepper

small piece root ginger, peeled and shredded

1 clove garlic, crushed

1 onion, finely chopped

1 small red pepper, seeded, cored and sliced thinly

3 tablespoons light soy sauce

1 tablespoon oil

1 tablespoon sugar

2 tablespoons sherry

1 tablespoon cornflour

300 ml (½ pint) chicken stock

Drain and mash the black beans. Mix with the salt, pepper, ginger, garlic, onion, pepper and soy sauce.

Heat the oil in a saucepan over high heat. Pour in the black bean mixture, reduce heat to medium and cook, stirring, for 4 minutes.

Blend the sugar, sherry and cornflour to a smooth cream and mix in with the stock. Stir the stock mixture into the pan and cook gently, stirring, until thickened slightly. Simmer, covered, for 25 minutes. Serve hot with the Sesame spareribs.

Note: Salted black beans are available from Chinese supermarkets.

✳ Freeze for up to 2 months. To serve, thaw for 2 hours at room temperature then heat in a saucepan over low heat.

≈ Microwave on DEFROST for 5 minutes, stirring once. Microwave on HIGH for 2–3 minutes until hot, stirring twice.

Bitter Coffee Caramels

SERVES 4

150 g (5 oz) sugar

85 ml (3 fl oz) water

2 eggs, beaten

1 teaspoon instant coffee blended with a few drops of boiling water

300 ml (½ pint) milk

Oven temperature: 160°C (325°F), Gas Mark 3
Place 100 g (4 oz) of the sugar in a small, heavy-based saucepan with the water. Stir, over low heat, until the sugar has dissolved. Bring to the boil; continue boiling until the syrup turns a light golden brown

colour. Pour most of the caramel into four greased ramekin dishes and turn them to coat the sides evenly. Pour the remaining caramel on to a greased baking sheet and leave to set hard.

Whisk the eggs lightly with the coffee solution and the remaining sugar. Pour the milk into a small saucepan and heat gently until tepid. Whisk the milk into the eggs. Strain the mixture through a sieve on to the caramel in the ramekin dishes.

Place the dishes in a shallow baking pan. Pour in enough warm water to come halfway up their sides. Bake for about 30–40 minutes or until set. Remove the dishes, cool and chill overnight.

To serve, roughly crush the caramel on the baking sheet with the end of a rolling pin.

Loosen the caramels from the dishes with the point of a knife. Turn out on to serving plates and top each with a little crushed caramel.

Serving suggestion: Provide small biscuits, such as Langue de chat, to eat with the dessert.

✳ Not suitable for freezing.

Above Bitter coffee caramels served with small biscuits

· INDEX ·

110

.ACKNOWLEDGEMENTS.

Photography by Grant Symon. Except the following: p.40 by Robert Golden, p.44 by Theo Bergström, p.96 by Paul Bussell

Photographic styling by Hilary Guy and Penny Markham

Food prepared for photography by Maureen Pogson, Judy Bugg, Eve Dowling, Allyson Birch, Stella Murphy and Jackie Baxter

Illustrations by Hayward and Martin Limited

Editors: Eve Dowling and Linda Seward
Art Director: Alyson Kyles
Designer: Alicia Howard